Be patient,
God hasn't finished with me yet!

Be patient,
God hasn't finished
with me yet!

Learning from the life of Jacob

Roger Ellsworth

 EVANGELICAL PRESS

EVANGELICAL PRESS
Faverdale North Industrial Estate, Darlington, DL3 0PH, England

Evangelical Press USA
P. O. Box 84, Auburn, MA 01501, USA

e-mail: sales@evangelicalpress.org
web: http://www.evangelicalpress.org

First published 2003

British Library Cataloguing in Publication Data available

ISBN 0 85234 524 0

Other books by Roger Ellsworth

31 days of Christmas	How to live in a dangerous world
Apostasy, destruction and hope	Journey to the cross
Faithful under fire	A promise is a promise
From glory to ruin	The Shepherd King
The Guide — Bible book by book	Strengthening Christ's church
He is altogether lovely	

Printed and bound in Great Britain by Creative Print and Design Wales, Ebbw Vale, South Wales.

The following pages are dedicated to

Bob Hutchens,
encourager and friend

Acknowledgements

The following chapters were first presented in sermon form to the dear saints of Immanuel Baptist Church. I thank God for their keen interest in the Word of God and for their constant encouragement to me to 'preach the Word'. I also appreciate the kind assistance of my secretary Laura Simmons, and the staff of Evangelical Press in preparing these chapters for publication. Special thanks go to my wife Sylvia for her constant and gentle pressure on me to write.

Contents

Introduction

It must seem to many to be an astonishing thing for an author to ask his readers to join him in a study of the life of Jacob. Jacob lived a very long time ago. There were no computers. Jacob did not send or receive e-mail. There were no television sets, no VCRs, and no cars.

What possible value is there, then, in studying the life of a man so far removed from our own sophisticated times? I offer three primary reasons we should engage in such a study.

Jacob's life is recorded in the Word of God

First, we study the life of Jacob simply because it is in the Bible. The Bible is a special book. It was not written as other books. The books of the Bible were written by men who were inspired by the Holy Spirit of God (2 Tim. 3:16; 2 Peter 1:21).

Because of the Bible's special character, everything it says is of vital importance. After affirming that all Scripture is inspired by God, the apostle Paul says it is 'profitable for doctrine, for reproof, for correction, for instruction in right-eousness, that the man of God may be complete, thoroughly equipped for every good work' (2 Tim. 3:16-17).

This profit can be derived, of course, from the lives of the men and women which Scripture records. These lives are not here merely to furnish us with academic information. They are here because they illustrate vital spiritual truths that can be of immense value to us.

The Holy Spirit included many examples in Scripture because they speak very powerfully and forcefully to us. The Puritan Thomas Brooks recognized this and wrote: 'Example is the most powerful rhetoric.'[1] John MacArthur adds: 'The single greatest tool of spiritual leadership is the power of an exemplary life... We are better at following a pattern or a model than we are at fleshing out a precept or principle.'[2]

But just what role does Jacob play in Scripture? Why is his story in the Bible? Before we can answer such questions, we must raise another; that is, what kind of book is the Bible? Is it simply a collection of stories, thoughts, poems, sermons and various moral instructions? Or is it more?

No less an authority than the Lord Jesus Christ himself speaks on this matter. He specifically asserted on more than one occasion that the Bible is a book about himself and the eternal salvation he came to this earth to provide for his people (Luke 24:27, 44). That theme sounds very early in Scripture (Gen. 3:15), and it continues to sound until the very end. Jacob's story is in the Bible because it moves this theme forward, as we shall soon see.

Every Christian can identify with Jacob

A second reason for studying the life of Jacob is that every Christian can identify with him. We might say every Christian is named Jacob. My name is Jacob. I can see myself in him and him in me.

Abraham, Moses, Samuel, Daniel, Isaiah, Paul — all seem like towering peaks in the mountain range of Scripture. So often I dwell on a spiritual plateau. I do not seem able to ascend to the dizzying heights occupied by these wonderful stalwarts of the faith.

Then there is Jacob. Yes, he was a man of faith, so much so that we find him included among the heroes of the faith (Heb. 11:21). But it was a hard struggle for Jacob. It is apparent as we read about him that he was a deeply flawed man. In Jacob I see the twistedness, the sinfulness, of human nature.

Jacob was an immensely blessed man. The Lord had graciously chosen his grandfather Abraham to be the father of the nation of Israel. That was no small thing. The Jewish nation was to be the nation into which the Messiah was born. Jacob was, by the grace of God, Abraham's descendant and the one who would receive God's promises.

At the beginning Jacob did not prize the promises of God and did not cling to them in faith. In his early days, he was a man who was completely wrapped up in himself. His only concern was his own advancement. He was always biased towards self. In this self-centredness Jacob was willing to trample on those around him: his father, his brother, his uncle. Jacob would have made a good modern man. Look out for number one at all costs!

Jacob is indeed a picture of us all. We all come into this world with a nature that makes us oblivious to the things of God as we are engrossed in ourselves. Even those of us who come to know the Lord are never free from struggle against sin in this life.

Jacob's God is the God of all believers

That brings us to yet another reason to consider the life of Jacob: his God is the God of all who believe. Jacob's God is our God. He is what we might call the 'hero' of every story in the Bible. God is certainly the hero in the story of Jacob.

The sufficiency of God's grace

As we consider Jacob we shall find three gigantic truths about God emerging. Firstly, we shall see the sufficiency of his grace.

How grace shines and sparkles in the life of this man! Had it not been for the grace of God, Jacob would have remained a scoundrel and the account of his life would be nothing but a blot on the pages of history. But God had other plans.

Here we have in part, then, how the account of Jacob moves the Bible's theme of redemption forward. God's grace is the fountain from which redemption flows. Jacob is chosen and granted faith by that grace. He is changed and matured by it. He is nurtured and sustained by it. He is guided and protected by it. He is renewed by it.

It is a stubborn grace. It refuses to let Jacob go, even with all his infuriating flaws. It hangs on to him. It wrestles with him. And when he finally comes to the end of life, he is able to look back over his pilgrimage and admire what grace has done:

'God, before whom my fathers
    Abraham and Isaac walked,
The God who has fed me
    all my life long to this day,
The Angel who has redeemed
    me from all evil...'

(Gen. 48:15-16).

The word 'fed' should not be taken to refer only to temporal or physical food. It should actually be translated 'shepherded'. Jacob was declaring that the Lord had been his shepherd all along. God had provided for him and protected him. God had guided him.

It had been grace all the way for Jacob. If you were to cut his life anywhere it would bleed grace. Jacob's life is important for every child of God to ponder thoroughly because the very same thing can be said of us: it is grace all the way. Grace chose us. Grace saved us. Grace sanctifies us. Grace preserves us. Grace guides us. It is grace on top of grace for the child of God. It is grace all the way.

The certainty of God's purpose

The second major truth about God that emerges from the life of Jacob has to do with the certainty of his purpose.

Before Jacob was born, the Lord had made it clear that he, Jacob, would be the one who would receive the covenant promises (Gen. 25:23). It often seemed as if that would never actually happen. Jacob's father Isaac was determined that Esau should receive the covenant blessing. Then there were those times when it seemed as if the lives of Jacob and his family would be snuffed out and God's purpose would come crashing to the ground. When the time came for Jacob to die, he and his family were not even in the land of promise.

Yet through it all, God was at work, and not one word failed of anything he promised. Jacob did indeed receive the covenant blessing. His own life and the lives of his sons were preserved. And Israel did not get swallowed up in Egypt.

The certainty of God's promises

Thirdly, it is important for us to study the life of Jacob so that we too can rejoice in the certainty of God's promises. We live in such wicked and evil times that it often seems as if the cause of God is going to fail. But it will not fail! The same God who prevailed in the life of Jacob will prevail in our situation. He is not defeated by the evil of men. His will is not thwarted by popular opinion. Let hell rage and gather as a flood. Let the kingdom of evil swagger and bluster. All kingdoms will perish, and the kingdom of God will remain. And one glorious day every knee will bend before the Lord of this universe, the Lord Jesus Christ, and every single tongue will confess that he is indeed Lord.

Only those who are on the right side of the Lord in this life will be on the right side of him when that glorious moment comes. Those who are on the wrong side then will hear these terribly solemn words: '...I never knew you; depart from me...' (Matt. 7:23).

The piercing question, then, is how to get on the right side of Christ in this life. The answer is clear. The same grace that worked in the life of Jacob works today. Through that grace, and that grace alone, we can, as Jacob himself did, become utterly ashamed of our sinfulness, repent of it, and cast ourselves entirely upon the Lord Jesus Christ as our Lord and Saviour.

1.
A hard struggle with clear truth

Genesis 25:19-28

It has been rather popular in recent years to treat Isaac and Rebekah and their sons as a picture of the modern-day dysfunctional family. We may very well be able to gain lessons for family living from Isaac's family, but we mishandle this portion of Scripture if we see nothing more.

Isaac's family was not like any other. God had a special claim on them. He had called Isaac's father Abraham out of idolatry in the land of Ur and had made astounding promises to him. He had promised that Abraham would be the father of a great nation, and that through that nation all the families of the earth would be blessed (Gen. 12:1-3).

How were all other nations to be blessed through Abraham and his descendants? One of his descendants was to be the Messiah himself. God would take our humanity upon himself and in that humanity would provide forgiveness of sins and eternal salvation for his people, that is, those who would share the faith of Abraham.

Isaac, as the only son of Abraham and his wife Sarah, was the one who had been chosen to receive the promises God had made to his father. What a blessing he had received!

God speaks

Now it was time for Isaac himself to be a father. After years
of waiting, his wife Rebekah had conceived. It should have
been a very happy time, but Rebekah was feeling anxious.
She was carrying twins, and the Bible says 'the children strug-
gled together within her' (v. 22).

Rebekah did what every child of God should do with his
or her troubles. She took them to the Lord. The hymn, 'What
a Friend we have in Jesus', puts before us the wisdom of acting
in the same way as Rebekah:

> Oh, what peace we often forfeit,
> Oh, what needless pain we bear
> All because we do not carry
> Everything to God in prayer.

The Lord graciously answered Rebekah's prayer by giving this
explanation:

> 'Two nations are in your womb,
> Two peoples shall be separated from your body;
> One people shall be stronger than the other,
> And the older shall serve the younger'

(v. 23).

We may rest assured that Rebekah revealed the content of
this divine revelation to Isaac. Therefore both Rebekah and
Isaac must have known before their two sons were born that
God, in exercising his sovereign prerogative, was placing the
younger of the two sons, Jacob, over the older, Esau. That
would mean, among other things, that the Messiah would
spring from Jacob's line, not from Esau's. So Esau himself

would have to embrace the revelation of God concerning his brother.

Why would God do such a thing? Why would he place the second child over the first? Why would he place the weaker over the stronger? In other cultures it was a foregone conclusion that the firstborn would have priority. Why did God insist on reversing this pattern?

The answer is found in what we have already noted. Isaac's family was different. It was the family of the Messiah and the salvation he, the Messiah, would provide. When we look at Isaac's family, then, we must do so through this particular lens. They are not just another husband and wife and children struggling to understand and get along with each other.

By placing Jacob, the second child, over Esau, the Lord was driving home the essential nature of salvation. He was showing that it is entirely a matter of his doing. Jacob had done nothing to deserve being set over Esau. Esau had done nothing to deserve being set aside. Jacob was elevated solely because it pleased God to do so. It was sheer grace. There was absolutely nothing for which Jacob could take credit. He could not explain his elevation by saying he was stronger than Esau. He was not. He could not explain it in terms of being wiser than Esau. He proved to be, but God placed him above Esau while the two of them were still in the womb. We cannot attribute wisdom to Jacob at that stage!

God has always liked to act in this particular way. He has always delighted in elevating the weak and foolish over the strong and the wise. When Israel needed a king, God bypassed all the more impressive sons of Jesse and settled on unimpressive David (1 Sam. 16). When God sent his Son into this world, he bypassed Jerusalem, the religious, cultural and political centre of that region, and settled on tiny, unimpressive Bethlehem. When Jesus chose his twelve disciples, he bypassed the movers and shakers of the day, the elite of society, and settled on some fishermen, a tax-collector and a political zealot or two. The apostle Paul affirms that God operates in the very same way in this matter of eternal salvation. As a general rule, he bypasses the wise, the mighty and the noble, and settles on the foolish, the weak and the base (1 Cor. 1:26-28).

You can be absolutely sure that salvation is the result of God's grace just as much as Jacob's elevation (Rom. 9:10-13). It is not a matter of our meriting it or our working for it. It is all the product of the grace of God. It is God who chooses, calls and grants repentance and faith. If we love him, it is because he first loved us. There is not one shred of credit that a saved person can take for himself. All the glory goes to the Lord.

How sinful human nature resists this teaching! But while we resist, the Bible insists. Just as the Lord God chose Jacob, so he has chosen each of his people. The apostle Paul affirms this in these breathtaking words: 'Blessed be the God and Father of our Lord Jesus Christ, who has blessed us with every spiritual blessing in the heavenly places in Christ, just as he chose us in him before the foundation of the world, that we should be holy and without blame before him in love, having predestined us to adoption as sons by Jesus Christ to himself, according to the good pleasure of his will, to the praise of the glory of his grace, by which he made us accepted in the Beloved' (Eph. 1:3-6).

We have here the *fact* of election: 'He chose us'. Here we have its *time*: 'before the foundation of the world'; its *basis*: 'according to the good pleasure of his will'; and its *vehicle*: 'in Christ'. Here also is its *purpose*: 'that we should be holy and without blame before him in love'. And here is the proper *response* to it: 'to the praise of the glory of his grace'.

We may quibble all we want about why the Lord would operate in this way, but whether we like it or not, this is his way, as he made abundantly clear in his revelation to Rebekah.

Isaac resists

Isaac, for one, did not care much for God's revelation. He preferred Esau over Jacob, and, as we shall note later, was determined that Esau should be set over Jacob. Isaac was pleased enough that God had singled out his father Abraham to receive his covenant. He had no trouble with God placing him over his half-brother Ishmael to receive this same covenant. But he stumbled over the thought of God placing Jacob over Esau.

What was the reason for Isaac's preference for Esau? The account tells us that Esau was a skilful hunter (v. 27) and that Isaac loved him 'because he ate of his game' (v. 28). This is a statement of immense and staggering proportions. The issue at hand was spiritual in nature. As we have noted, it had to do with God's covenant, which included the promise of eternal salvation through the coming Messiah.

Yet all Isaac could think about was his stomach! He was willing to set aside God's clear revelation because of his interest in the temporal and perishing. There was, of course, nothing wrong with him loving Esau. Every father should love his son. But there was something wrong with him allowing that love to obscure and override what God had revealed regarding Esau. It was fine for Isaac to love Esau, but it was not fine for him to desire for Esau what God had reserved for Jacob.

Isaac's struggle to embrace the Word of God at this point speaks very pointedly to all of us who know the Lord. We have, as Isaac had, a clear word from God. We have it in Scripture. That word often binds and constrains us. It calls us, as with Isaac, to give priority to its demands, to let it direct our loves. It calls upon us to lay aside our own comforts and desires in order to embrace what it has to say. It calls us to responsibilities that we find very difficult, speaking to us about putting our fleshly appetites and concerns over spiritual and eternal things. It says, '...seek those things which are above... Set your mind on things above, not on things on the earth' (Col. 3:1-2).

The example of Isaac should give each and every child of God occasion to examine himself. How are we responding to the clear teachings of God's Word? Are we giving priority to its demands? Are we letting it direct our loves? Or are we like Isaac, putting our desires and our comforts above the Word?

Eventually Isaac came to embrace the Word of God regarding Jacob and Esau (Gen. 28:1-4). He came to understand that God's way of doing things, while it may be difficult to understand and accept, is best. But what misery and havoc he brought into his family while he was struggling to learn that lesson!

We can either learn Isaac's lesson from Isaac himself or we can learn it, as he did, from hard and bitter experience.

2.
The 'Esau flaw'[1]

Genesis 25:29-34

One of the characteristics of our age is instant gratification, that is, living for the present. In Esau we have a perfect example of this kind of mentality. Esau sold his birthright to his brother Jacob in order to satisfy his hunger.

The birthright

If we are to understand the action of Esau, we must begin with the birthright. The firstborn son held a position of special prominence in most of the cultures of that time. Not only was he next to his parents in honour and authority, but the legal continuation of the family line was reckoned through him. Furthermore, he received a double portion of his father's inheritance. For instance, if a man had two sons, his estate would be divided into three parts and the older son would receive two. If there were three sons, the estate would be divided into four parts and again the oldest son would receive two.

While the birthright brought special honour and privileges in all the nations of that time, it should have had even more significance for Esau and Jacob. God had made a special covenant with their grandfather Abraham (Gen. 12:1-3). That covenant not only included the promise that the land of Canaan would belong to Abraham's descendants, but it also carried the promised that a Redeemer, the Messiah himself, would spring from Abraham's seed. These promises were part and parcel of the birthright.

There were, then, two aspects of the birthright, the physical and the spiritual, and these aspects made it a most glorious and blessed privilege. Neither Jacob nor Esau rightly prized the birthright. Judging from the interest he later manifested in material prosperity, we are probably justified in saying Jacob's interest in the birthright was motivated more by the material aspect of possessing the land of Canaan rather than by the spiritual aspect. Jacob, of course, came to prize the spiritual aspect, but that was years later.

The bargain

But if Jacob prized only part of the birthright, it is obvious that Esau prized none of it, and that brings us to consider the bargain he made.

Esau and Jacob were as different as any two men can be. Esau was a man of the outdoors and a sportsman. If he were around today, he would either be engaged in sports, talking about sports, or watching sports on TV, and would have the women swooning over him. Jacob, on the other hand, was a plain, mild-mannered man who despised physical exertion and relied on his wits to get ahead.

On the day described in this passage, the personalities of Esau and Jacob come through powerfully. Esau has been hunting, while Jacob has been at home cooking a stew. With his shrewd ability to think things out, to plan ahead and to discern how others would react in a given situation, it is entirely likely that Jacob had planned for this occasion. He knew Esau was a man of impulse who did not really value his birthright and that he would return from his hunt so famished that he would do anything for food. So Jacob made sure he had a hearty stew cooked to perfection and waiting for Esau.

When Esau arrived on the scene it was immediately obvious to Jacob that he had planned well. Sure enough, Esau was famished and did not waste any time demanding some of the stew, and Jacob wasted no time in offering Esau the deal he had hatched: the stew in exchange for the birthright. Quick as a flash, Esau agreed, ate the stew and walked away.

The significance of the bargain

The deal itself actually had no bearing on the eventual possession of the birthright. We find later that Isaac was still planning to give the blessing of the firstborn to Esau, and that required Jacob and his mother to have to do some more shrewd manoeuvring. But the deal Jacob and Esau made did accurately reflect the priorities and the character of these two men. It revealed Jacob's deceitfulness — a trait God worked long and hard to purge from him — and it revealed a terrible and tragic flaw in Esau.

What was Esau's flaw? Why did he so lightly regard something of such tremendous value? The answer is that he was a man who lived for the moment. The birthright to him was something distant and shadowy, something that might never be realized at all. His hunger, on the other hand, was there and then, real and pressing. He says, 'Look, I am about to die; so what is this birthright to me?' (v. 32).

That was, of course, a monstrous exaggeration. Esau was not in imminent danger of starvation, as his words implied.

Anybody who can still walk is strong enough to wait for a meal to be prepared. But the point is, that is how Esau felt at that particular moment, and that feeling was all that mattered to him. The Scottish preacher Hugh Black says of Esau, 'He feels he is going to die, as a man of his type is always sure he will die if he does not get what he wants when the passion is on him.'[2] The passion of the moment is all that counts! Instant gratification — that was Esau's mindset, and it is the mindset of many today.

But it is not enough for us to be able to isolate and identify the fallacy that crippled Esau's thinking. We must apply Esau's bargain to ourselves and ask if we are repeating it.

There is, of course, no shortage of applications to be made here. Instant gratification is as much a driving force with us as it was with Esau. Young people feel sexual passion and allow the feeling of that moment to cause them to disregard the dreadful disease of AIDS that may spring upon them a few years later, not to mention the guilt and loss of self-respect that often come only moments later. The businessman sees the chance to get ahead if he just engages in a little sharp dealing. So he allows the desire of that moment, the desire to be successful and to have financial security, to obscure completely the possibility of an indictment for fraud. The young married couple find the desire for things to be so compelling that they plunge head over heels into debt and recklessly disregard the bankruptcy that awaits them down the way. The college student plunges the drug needle into his arm because he cannot say 'No' to the intense craving of the moment, and he completely shuts out of his mind the forthcoming ruin of his health and wealth.

Much of the knack of living happily and successfully is tied to keeping firmly in mind the future consequences of present choices. But this generation has a terrifically hard time doing this and often falls into the 'Esau flaw' — living for the moment and hoping the future will take care of itself.

The most tragic manifestation of the 'Esau flaw'

This trap, as can easily be seen from the examples I have cited, can catch us in a variety of ways, but the most tragic of all is when we barter our eternal souls for the gratification of the moment.

The gospel of Jesus Christ is much like the birthright Esau squandered. It offers us benefits that are unseen, intangible, distant and shadowy. It says that if we will bow before Jesus Christ as our Lord and Saviour we shall receive God's forgiveness for our sins, the Holy Spirit of God will take up residence in us to guide us and cause us to mature in the things of God, and when this life is over we shall be ushered into the presence of God and the glories of heaven. But forgiveness of sin cannot be seen or touched. And neither can the Holy Spirit. And heaven may be out there somewhere, but as far as many are concerned it is at best a distant reality. This is the mind of Esau at work, and when the gospel comes with its glorious offers, the thinking of Esau has a way of coming in and taking over. Millions have done, and are doing, with the gospel the very same thing that Esau did with the birthright. They have turned their backs on it and walked away from it so they could eat some delicacy that the world has to offer, which can only satisfy for a moment.

If you are one who is about to sell your soul for the sake of some momentary gratification, I urge you to weigh the questions of Jesus about this very matter: 'For what profit is it to a man if he gains the whole world, and loses his own soul? Or what will a man give in exchange for his soul?' (Matt. 16:26).

Look at all this world has to offer and then look at the vast, boundless reaches of an eternity that will be spent either in heaven or hell. Are you ready to trade the eternal well-being of your soul in heaven for something that brings only temporary gratification? That is exactly what you do when you stop your ears against the gospel and walk away.

The author of Hebrews tells us that Esau came to regret his decision only after it was too late to do anything about it. He says, 'For you know that afterward, when he wanted to inherit the blessing, he was rejected, for he found no place for repentance, though he sought it diligently with tears' (Heb. 12:17).

I hope you will not repeat Esau's tragic blunder but that you will understand how inestimably precious the gospel is and will embrace it before it is too late. Do not let the passions and appetites of the moment blind you to eternal realities. Those realities may seem dim and distant now, but they will become real and present much sooner than you think.

3.
Inadequate responses to the Word of God

Genesis 27

We must rank the chapter before us as one of the saddest in the Bible. Here we have human conflict and distrust in very raw form. Husband is arrayed against wife, and wife against husband. Parents are arrayed against sons, and sons against parents. Brother is arrayed against brother. And, tragedy of tragedies, the people involved here profess to be in a special covenant relationship with God! How unbelievably sad it is when the people of God are ranged against each other! How much harm has been done to the kingdom of Christ by professing Christians allowing themselves to get caught in the same web of deceit and conflict that we find in this chapter! Perhaps God will be pleased to use the sordid details recorded here to renew in us the resolve to stand firm against such things.

As we look at this chapter, we shall see the price each party paid for their self-serving schemes.

The sinful scheming of Isaac and Esau (vv. 1-4)

Isaac knew from the beginning that his second son Jacob was to have priority over the firstborn, Esau. This meant that Jacob was to receive the covenant blessing from his father.

This was God's revealed truth, and it was not Isaac's place either to question or dispute it, but to submit to it. He was to embrace the Word of God and to honour it by bestowing the covenant blessing on Jacob.

But Isaac was unwilling to do this, and, shockingly, as this chapter opens we find him preparing to give the covenant blessing to Esau. S. G. DeGraaf pointedly says of Isaac: 'At times Isaac's faith sank dangerously low.'[1] Of the episode before us, DeGraaf writes: 'At this stage, Isaac was involved in a battle of the flesh against the Word of the Lord.'[2]

It is very interesting that Isaac sets in motion his plan to bless Esau by asking his son to first hunt game and make him the 'savoury food' that he, Isaac, loved (v. 4). Even Isaac was placing his palate over spiritual concerns.

Esau was eager, of course, to co-operate with his father. He had sold his birthright to Jacob, but he did not consider that bargain to be binding. He knew the blessing of his father was the thing that really mattered. Esau had finally come to the point where he earnestly desired that covenant blessing. But he still had no interest in the spiritual realities tied to it. No, Esau was too much a man of the here and now for that. His interest in the blessing flowed from his desire for the temporal and material advantages that it would bring to him.

The plan seemed foolproof. Esau would hunt game and prepare his father a meal, and his father would bestow the covenant blessing. All this would be done secretly and quickly. Esau would be recognized as the recipient of the covenant blessing before Rebekah and Jacob knew what had happened.

The sinful scheming of Rebekah and Jacob (vv. 5-29)

Things did not go as Isaac and Esau planned. Rebekah, knowing Isaac's preference for Esau and suspecting that he might undertake such a plan, made sure she lingered around his

tent every time Esau entered it. Her vigilance was rewarded
on this occasion. She heard Isaac and Esau's plot and immediately came up with a scheme of her own. Jacob would
pretend to be Esau and would receive the blessing instead.

The fact that Isaac was blind gave Rebekah and Jacob the
opportunity to deceive him, but this was still no small undertaking. Rebekah would have to make the savoury food Isaac
loved from goats' meat (vv. 9-10). And Jacob, to resemble
the hairiness of his brother, would have to wear hairy garments as he took the dish to his father (vv. 11-17).

The already sordid details of this deceitful scheme become
more sickening. Jacob, clothed in hairy garments, carries the
meat to his father and immediately begins to add one flagrant lie to another. He tells his blind father that he is Esau
(vv. 18-19). He claims that his goat meat is wild game that he
found very quickly through the help of the Lord (vv. 19-20).
In response to his father's question as to whether he really is
Esau, he says, 'I am' (vv. 21-24).

Although Isaac was clearly bewildered and mystified by
the disparity between the voice of Jacob and the hairiness
and smell of Esau, he went ahead and pronounced the cov-
eted blessing (vv. 27-29). Rebekah and Jacob's foul deed was
done. When Esau arrived, he and his father soon realized that
they had been hoodwinked. Isaac, trembling 'exceedingly'
(v. 33), said to Esau, 'Your brother came with deceit and has
taken away your blessing' (v. 35).

Is it really correct to attribute sin to Rebekah and Jacob in
this situation? Could it not rather be said that they were only
seeking to bring God's will to pass? It was, after all, God himself who had promised that Jacob would be elevated over
Esau. Could we not say, then, that Rebekah and Jacob were
merely helping God along? Did the end, the blessing of Jacob,
not justify the means, the deceiving of Isaac?

There can be no doubt about this issue. Rebekah and Jacob
were just as guilty of sinning in this situation as were Isaac

and Esau. While the latter were guilty of trying to set the Word of God aside so they could achieve their own desires, the former were guilty of failing to trust that same Word.

While Isaac and Esau believed God's Word was not authoritative, that indeed it could safely be ignored and set aside, Rebekah and Jacob believed it was not sufficient, that is, that God did not have the power and wisdom to carry out what he himself had promised!

We do not know how God would have carried out his word regarding Jacob and Esau. As we look at Isaac's plan to bless Esau, it seems, as it did to Rebekah and Jacob, that the promise of God was hanging by a thread and perilously close to crumbling. But God's Word is to be trusted even when it appears to be foolish to do so. Had Rebekah and Jacob been content merely to trust the Lord and wait upon him, they would have found his promise to be utterly secure and Jacob would have been elevated over Esau without having to resort to sinful scheming and trickery. We do not have to know how God would have brought it all to pass. It is not ours to know what God has reserved for himself. It is rather ours to trust what he has clearly revealed.

God has determined that all his promises and gifts are to be possessed, not by human effort, but rather by faith. Rebekah failed to realize this, and we can as well. Eternal salvation through the redeeming work of God's Son, Jesus Christ, is the greatest of all God's promises. And it is possessed only by faith. Those who seek to secure it by good works will find that they are not ready to stand before God at all (Matt. 7:21-23).

So Isaac, Rebekah, Esau and Jacob all failed to respond adequately to the Word of God, and all paid a fearful price. Isaac and Rebekah saw their already fragmented family divided further. The intense hatred of Esau for his brother caused

Isaac and Rebekah to send Jacob to stay with Laban, Rebekah's brother (v. 43). In all likelihood Rebekah never saw Jacob again. The 'few days' (v. 44) they anticipated turned into twenty long years, and when Jacob finally returned his father Isaac was still alive, but there is no mention of Rebekah (35:27-29).

Isaac and Rebekah also saw Esau turn even more decisively and dramatically against the covenant of God. Instead of embracing God's will concerning his brother, Esau allowed himself to be filled with hatred and rage. He further expressed his disdain for the spiritual aspect of the covenant by being willing to marry women who had no connection with Abraham. Esau's rejection of spiritual concerns was so complete that he became one of the Bible's emblems for a tragic lost state.

Jacob also paid for his inadequate response to the Word of God. We might say the Lord enrolled him in the school of spiritual maturity. In that school Jacob faced many hardships and learned some very painful but needed lessons.

All of this should make us examine ourselves and how we respond to the Word of God. Do we associate ourselves on this matter with Isaac and Esau by seeking to set aside God's Word in favour of our own desires? Or are we more like Rebekah and Jacob by failing to trust the Word of God while professing to desire and revere it?

This episode offers us another line of application as well. As God designated Jacob to receive the covenant blessing and to be the covenant head of the family, so he has designated the Lord Jesus Christ as the only way of eternal salvation. All of Isaac and Esau's scheming could not overthrow God's choice of Jacob, and nothing can overthrow Christ as God's way of salvation. If we are to receive this salvation, we must throw down our weapons and our schemes, and gladly embrace Jesus Christ as our Lord and Saviour.

4.
Jacob's dream at Bethel

Genesis 28:10-22

Jacob must have been a deeply troubled and beaten man as he made camp outside the village of Luz, forty-five miles away from his home. By this time he almost certainly would have replayed in his mind a thousand times the tape of what he had done, with each playing bringing him a more intense feeling of revulsion. He had deceived his father and cheated his brother. And now, to avoid Esau's murderous rage he was on his way to his Uncle Laban's house in faraway Padan Aram.

Before allowing Jacob to begin his journey, his father Isaac had bestowed yet another blessing upon him:

'May God Almighty bless you,
And make you fruitful and multiply you,
That you may be an assembly of peoples;
And give you the blessing of Abraham,
To you and your descendants with you,
That you may inherit the land
In which you are a stranger,
Which God gave to Abraham'

(28:3-4).

The words of that blessing may have hit Jacob with the force of a sledgehammer. God would certainly want nothing to do with him. He was nothing like his grandfather Abraham. And now he was leaving the very land he was supposed to inherit.

As Jacob made his bed on that particular night, he surely thought that he had nullified all God's promises and that heaven was closed to him for ever. Little did he realize the difference that night would make! As he slept, he dreamed a dream that was like no other. He saw a ladder extending from earth to heaven with the angels of God ascending and descending on it and with God himself standing above it.

The ladder from earth to heaven

Let us consider the three parts of this vision. First, consider the ladder from earth to heaven.

How thrilling it was for Jacob to see that ladder! Heaven was not closed to him! Even though he was nothing more than a vile sinner who had flagrantly disobeyed the laws of God, he could still enter heaven. The door was open to him.

Jacob certainly did not deserve to enter heaven. He would have had no reason to complain if God had given him a quite different dream — one in which there was no ladder at all between heaven and earth; one in which the gates of heaven were barred and chained and guarded with scowling angels.

A holy God does not owe guilty sinners anything at all. He does not have to open his heaven to them. He would be entirely justified if he were to leave heaven closed and sinners in their sins. But because this holy God is also gracious, he has made it possible for sinners to be forgiven and to enter into his heaven. To say that God is gracious is to acknowledge that he has done everything necessary for us to be saved. He has shouldered the whole load in this matter of salvation.

It is striking that God revealed this ladder while Jacob was sleeping. Up to this point Jacob's philosophy of life could be expressed by the proverb, 'The Lord helps those who help themselves.' He regarded the blessing of God upon his life as something that he had to secure through his own ingenuity and effort. But God revealed this ladder to heaven, not while Jacob was exerting himself, but while he was sleeping. In that condition Jacob could do nothing but receive what God was revealing. This stands in stark contrast to the tower builders who thought that they could reach heaven through their own efforts (Gen. 11:1-9).

We must not dismiss Jacob's dream as a piece of meaningless antiquity. The issue that God was dealing with in this dream is just as real and pressing as it was on that occasion. We are all by nature sinners as Jacob was, and we all must wonder, as he did, whether we will be able to enter heaven. Thank God that there is a ladder between earth and heaven. That ladder is none other than the Lord Jesus Christ himself, who confirmed this when he applied Jacob's experience to himself (John 1:51).

Jesus Christ is the only way for sinners to enter into heaven. By his perfect obedience to God's laws, he provided the righteousness sinners need to enter heaven. By his death on Calvary's cross he received the penalty for their sins. Christ, who had no sins of his own, took our sins, and we, who had no righteousness of our own, receive his righteousness (2 Cor. 5:21). What Christ did for sinners becomes ours by faith, and Christ's redeeming work is such that even foul sinners like Jacob can be forgiven and cleansed.

Phillip Henry describes the type of ladder we find in the Lord Jesus Christ. He is the *living* ladder. He is a *long* ladder, reaching all the way from earth to heaven. He is a *lasting* ladder, one that never wears out. He is a *free* ladder, open to all who come to him. He is a *firm* ladder, unshaken and

unshakeable. He is a *fitted* ladder, sufficient to every purpose for which he was intended and for every need of his
people.[1]

The angels on the ladder

But how do we know Christ is the way of salvation? How do
we know he is the ladder? To answer that question, we must
look at the second part of Jacob's dream, the angels ascending
and descending on the ladder.

Jesus promised Nathanael that he would see the angels of
God ascending and descending upon him, the Lord Jesus
Christ (John 1:51). Angels did indeed attend the ministry of
the Lord Jesus, and the disciples saw them on occasions (Luke
24:4-5; Acts 1:11). But even when they did not see angels
themselves, the disciples saw the signature of heaven upon
Jesus' ministry. Jesus healed the sick, raised the dead, cast
out demons. He stilled the water, multiplied loaves and fish,
and turned water into wine. He fulfilled over three hundred
Old Testament prophecies. Best of all, Jesus himself arose
from the grave on the third day and forty days later ascended
to the Father in heaven. What are these but proofs that the
angels of God were attending his ministry and that he was
indeed, as he claimed, the Son of God from heaven itself?

Those who doubt that Jesus is God's way of salvation,
God's ladder from earth to heaven, should especially consider
the cumulative weight of these proofs. One or two might be
explained away, but how does one explain them all away?
Together they are overwhelming.

We might think of it in terms of this illustration from
Robert A. Laidlaw: 'Take ten identical coins and mark them
one to ten. Place them in your pocket. Now take one out. There
is one chance in ten that you will get number one. Now replace

it, and the chances that number two will follow number one are not one in ten, but one in one hundred. With each new coin taken out, the risk will be multiplied by ten, so that the chance of ten following nine is one in ten billion.'[2]

We might say one of the evidences for Christ is like pulling the first coin out of the pocket. But all the evidences would be like pulling all ten coins out in sequence. That is staggering in its significance.

The Lord above the ladder

The final part of Jacob's dream was the Lord standing above the ladder. What a wonderful picture this is! The Lord was there to bless Jacob. How he blessed Jacob! After indicating that he would, in the words of Matthew Henry, 'be the same'[3] to him as he had been to Abraham and Isaac, the Lord proceeded to give him these specific promises:

- 'I am with you'
- 'I will keep you wherever you go'
- 'I will bring you back to this land'
- 'I will not leave you until I have done what I have spoken to you'

(v. 15).

In each of the promises there is a parallel in the lives of all God's people. The Lord has promised to be with his people (Matt. 28:20). He has promised to keep them, so much so that not one shall ever perish (1 Peter 1:5; Jude 24). He has also promised to bring them into their own land, that is, into heaven itself (John 14:1-3; Phil. 3:20-21). And he has promised that he will not fail to deliver unto his people everything that he has promised (Phil. 1:6; Heb. 13:5).

The Lord who stands above the ladder to pour every spiritual blessing upon his people (Eph. 1:3-14) also stands there to receive them when they finally leave this world. What a glorious day that will be!

When Jacob awoke he responded to the glorious dream by expressing surprise and wonder (vv. 16-17), by setting up a monument (v. 18), by naming that place 'Bethel' (v. 19) and by committing a tenth of his income to the Lord (vv. 20-22).

All of these things indicate that Jacob was quite overwhelmed. He found it hard to believe that God would show such mercy to him. Everyone who has truly seen heaven's door standing open and Christ as the ladder to that open door will have some sense of awe and wonder. Everyone who truly sees Christ as the ladder and comes to him in faith will never be able to forget the experience. Everyone who truly comes to Christ will be committed to serving him.

If that desire to serve is missing from our lives we need to question whether we have ever seen the ladder.

5.

Jacob in God's school

Genesis 29-30

Jacob had to be one happy man as he left Bethel to continue his journey to Haran! There was a ladder from earth to heaven! Although he was a vile sinner indeed, there was forgiveness for him and acceptance by God. We should not doubt for a single moment that, through this dream, God made the promise of the coming Redeemer very real to Jacob. That Redeemer was the ladder, and, while Jacob had known about the promise of the Redeemer, he now rested in faith upon him.

Perhaps Jacob thought all his troubles were now over. He was wrong. God was not content to forgive Jacob of his sins and to assure him of entrance into heaven. He insisted on making him into the man he wanted him to be — a godly man who truly feared the Lord and served him faithfully.

J. I. Packer says of God's plan for Jacob, 'Jacob must be weaned away from trust in his own cleverness to dependence upon God, and must be made to abhor the unscrupulous double-dealing which came so natural to him. Jacob, therefore, must be made to feel his own utter weakness and foolishness, and brought to such complete self-distrust that he would no longer try to get on by exploiting others. Jacob's self-reliance must go, once and for all.'[1]

When Jacob left Bethel to continue his journey to Haran we might say that he was in fact journeying to school — God's school. Every Christian is enrolled in God's school. God does not just save us and then leave us to ourselves. He does not forgive us of our sins only to wave a fond farewell and say, 'I'll see you in heaven.' He rather sets to work upon us to bring us to maturity and growth, to wean us away from this world and from ourselves and to cast us more completely upon himself and his grace.

This is God's work or God's school of sanctification, and it is vital for all of us to understand that Christians do not register for this school. Some have the idea that they can take God's salvation and skip the school of sanctification. They are content to be 'carnal Christians', that is, be saved and live like the world. As far as they are concerned, this is the best of all options. They can go through life enjoying the pleasures of sin and then go to heaven when they die. They have the best of both worlds.

The problem with this is that it is a pipe dream with no foundation or basis in fact. God does not give us a choice about this matter of entering his school. He automatically registers all whom he saves.

The house of Laban proved to be a good school for Jacob. There he learned some very important and vital lessons.

To despise sin

Through association with Laban

In Laban, Jacob met his match. He met one who was as ruthless and deceptive as he, Jacob, had been. J. I. Packer says, 'Jacob's experience with Laban was a case of the biter bit: God used it to show Jacob what it was like to be at the receiving end of a swindle — something that Jacob needed to learn, if he was ever going to fall out of love with his own previous way of life.'[2]

Laban deceived Jacob on the matter of marriage. After agreeing that he would give his daughter Rachel in return for Jacob's seven years of labour (29:18), Laban gave him his other daughter Leah (29:21-26), and bamboozled Jacob into working yet another seven years for Rachel (29:27).

Jacob responded to Laban's deception with more deception. He shrewdly manipulated the breeding of Laban's livestock so that he, Jacob, was greatly enriched and Laban was not (30:25-43). The fact that Jacob responded in this way shows us that sin is not easily uprooted in our lives. God's school of sanctification does not end after a semester or two. It is lifelong.

There is not much joy in a life that consists of deceiving and being deceived, and we may be sure that even though Jacob had not yet completely abandoned his old practices, he became increasingly frustrated with them. God's school was achieving its purpose.

Through his wives and children

Another feature of Jacob's life during these years also contributed to him despising his sin, namely, the situation with his wives and children. While he was still at home, Jacob had a major hand in the fragmentation of his own family by deceiving his father and cheating his brother. He had been so wilful and selfish that he had lived without regard for others. He had let a spirit of ambition and rivalry override other concerns.

Now the boot is on the other foot. Jacob has two wives, and as his children begin to come into this world, he learns how painful rivalry and wilfulness in the family can be

(29:31 - 30:24). Rachel is so jealous of her sister Leah bearing Jacob children that she insists that Jacob take her handmaid Bilhah as his wife (30:1-8). Then when Leah stopped bearing, she, Leah, insisted that Jacob take *her* handmaid Zilpah as his wife (30:9-13).

The rivalry and jealously went back and forth to such a degree that Jacob most certainly became extremely weary of them and profoundly regretted that he himself had acted in a similar way.

To depend on God

God had promised Jacob that his descendants would be as the dust of the earth and that he would indeed return to the land of Canaan (28:14). While he was at Laban's house, Jacob began to see the fulfilment of the first of these promises. There he saw the birth of eleven sons, and a twelfth was born shortly after he left Laban (35:16-20).

All of this took place in the context of much sin and failure. Laban tricked Jacob into marrying Leah. Jacob ended up with two wives and two concubines, which was a violation of God's creation ordinance that a man should have only one wife (Gen. 2:24). And, as we have noted, there was a great deal of jealousy and rivalry in Jacob's home.

The fact that God fulfilled his promise of many descendants for Jacob shows that even human sin cannot thwart the plans and purposes of God. God is not the author of sin, and he certainly does not approve of sin, but he can even use the sinfulness of men to advance his plan.

The classic example of this comes later in the book of Genesis. Joseph, Jacob's favourite son, is sold into slavery by his brothers. In bringing this about, Joseph's brothers were guilty of terrible sin; but God, while not excusing their sin, used it to achieve his plan. Years later, Joseph said to his brothers: '...you meant evil against me; but God meant it for good, in order to bring it about as it is this day...' (Gen. 50:20).

We find another example of this in the New Testament. All four Gospels record how Judas Iscariot betrayed the Lord Jesus Christ. While God did not approve of Judas' sin, he made it an integral part of his plan to send his Son to the cross to provide eternal salvation for all who believe.

We must not conclude from this that we should sin so that God can use it in some way. God never condones sin, and it always brings ill consequences into our lives and the lives of others. The point is simply this: God cannot be defeated by our sins.

What a precious word this is! Sometimes sin appears to be so very powerful and the kingdom of Christ so very feeble. God's people have nothing to fear! Sin will never keep God from achieving the end he has appointed. The Lord Jesus will finally return. The Lord's people will finally be gathered home. And sin and Satan will then be defeated for ever.

After spending twenty years with Laban, Jacob received God's commandment to return to the land of Canaan (31:13). That may very well seem to be a small and inconsequential thing to us, but it was far from it. Laban pursued him. Jacob had no sooner dealt with that situation than he learned that Esau was on his way to meet him. But through it all, God brought Jacob back to the land of Canaan.

We do well if we allow Jacob's experiences to drive home this mighty truth: the Lord's Word is utterly dependable and trustworthy. Christians are called to live on the basis of that Word. It often seems foolish to do so. We are frequently being told that times have changed, and the Word of God is constantly attacked and ridiculed. But that Word will ultimately prove to be true. And when God's people are home in heaven, they will look back on their earthly sojourn and say, '...not one thing has failed of all the good which the LORD ... spoke. All have come to pass ... not one word of them has failed' (Josh. 23:14).

May God help us today to firmly believe that which will be the cause of such rejoicing in the future — the reliability of the Word of God.

6.
Glimpses of grace

Genesis 31

At first glance this chapter of Genesis does not seem to offer us much of value. It simply relates to us how Jacob came to depart from Laban's house after twenty years. There seems to be nothing here except more of the very things that had characterized Jacob's stay there: deception, misunderstanding and resentment.

A deeper look reveals that there is more here than first appears. The grace of God sparkles and shines in various ways in this chapter.

Guiding grace

First, we see the guiding grace of God. Although the Lord had distinctly promised to return him to the land of Canaan, Jacob often found himself wondering if he would ever see that land again. Twenty long years had passed, and he was still toiling away for this uncle. It must have seemed to Jacob that God had forgotten all about his promise. Jacob may very well have been tempted to do as he had done before, namely, to take matters into his own hands without waiting on God. Yet now, having been schooled by the Lord, he chose to wait.

Verse 3 tells us that Jacob's patience was finally rewarded: 'Then the LORD said to Jacob, "Return to the land of your fathers and to your family, and I will be with you."' God never forgets a promise, and he never fails to keep the promises he has made.

God's people today stand in need of his guidance as much as Jacob did. And God certainly still guides. The apostle Paul assures us of this with these words: 'For as many as are led by the Spirit of God, these are sons of God' (Rom. 8:14).

This verse provides much comfort to Christians who constantly vex themselves on the matter of whether they are 'in the perfect will of God'. It asserts that God's guidance is part and parcel of being a child of God. God guides us more than we realize!

How does God guide his people? He does so to some degree by giving them a deep, settled conviction in their hearts and through their circumstances. Jacob was certainly interpreting his circumstances when he took note of the attitude of Laban's sons (v. 1) and of Laban himself (v. 2). But the primary way God guided Jacob was through speaking to him, and this is still the case today. Unlike with Jacob, God speaks to us in the form of his written word. The primary way for us to find God's guidance, then, is through careful reading and study of the Word of God. Paul linked the leading of the Spirit with God's Word by writing: '...the sword of the Spirit ... is the word of God...' (Eph. 6:17).

Hidden grace

This chapter also gives us insight into what we might call the hidden grace of God. In his conversation with his wives, Jacob gives testimony to this aspect of the grace of God. As he looks back on his twenty years with Laban, he realizes that God had been there all along to provide and care for him. He says, '...the God of my father has been with me' (v. 5). Later on, he affirms that God had not allowed Laban to 'hurt' him (v. 7).

The most intriguing part of Jacob's testimony to the grace of God comes when he relates a dream in which God had spoken to him (vv. 11-13). In this dream the Lord informed Jacob that he had been providing for him all along. He takes Jacob back to an agreement that he and Laban had made, namely, that Jacob would take as payment all the speckled and spotted sheep in Laban's flocks (30:32-35). Jacob came up with a scheme he thought would produce a large number of speckled and spotted sheep (30:37-42). The fact that these sheep began to multiply in abundance (30:43) must have caused him no small amount of satisfaction. His scheme was working!

Jacob was in for a surprise. In his dream he learned that it was not his scheme that led to his blessing. It was rather because God had been supervising the whole process (v. 12). The speckled and spotted sheep flourished and abounded, not because Jacob had discovered some new breeding technique, but solely because God had determined to bless and enrich Jacob.

So Jacob was compelled to say to Leah and Rachel: 'So God has taken away the livestock of your father and given them to me' (v. 9). God had overruled both Laban's evil intent towards Jacob and Jacob's own scheming! We do not need to have a dream such as Jacob had to learn the truth it taught him, that is, that God is at work in the lives of his people to enrich and bless them even when it appears that he is not.

What burden is it that you carry this day? What difficulty befuddles and perplexes you? Does it seem that God has forsaken you? The fact that you cannot sense the grace of God in a given circumstance does not mean that it is not there. His grace is at work even in the midst of our difficulties. It works to strengthen us, to instruct us, and, yes, even to enrich us through the experience. It is often hidden, but it is real.

Jacob's son Joseph experienced God's hidden grace. In all likelihood, he saw no grace at all in being sold into slavery. He must have thought that God had utterly forsaken him. But God's grace was working in that situation, and at the end Joseph testified to that grace (Gen. 50:20).

From time to time we do, as Joseph did, get glimpses of grace that is for the most part hidden, but when we finally come to the end of life's journey and are in the presence of God, we shall find no hidden grace. All will then be abundantly and remarkably clear. And as we look back upon our earthly pilgrimage, we will gladly testify that God's grace was there all the time and that it led us all the way.

> When my spirit, clothed immortal,
> Wings its flight to realms of day,
> This my song through endless ages—
> Jesus led me all the way.[1]
>
> Fanny J. Crosby (1820-1915)

Preserving and protecting grace

This chapter also enables us to rejoice in the preserving and protecting grace of God. This aspect of God's grace was on display when Jacob actually departed from Laban's house. Waiting until Laban had gone away to shear sheep, Jacob began his journey to Canaan (vv. 20-22). Laban was not told about this until three days after Jacob had left and, enraged at Jacob's departure, hotly pursued him. He would later attribute his anger to not being able to bid his daughters and grandchildren a proper farewell (vv. 26-28), but it is more likely that he was angry about losing his top employee.

We have no way of knowing exactly what Laban was planning while he pursued Jacob. Perhaps he intended to bring him back by force. Whatever his designs, God stepped in to short-circuit them. During Laban's pursuit of Jacob, God appeared in a dream to Laban and said, 'Be careful that you speak to Jacob neither good nor bad' (v. 24). In other words, Laban was to say absolutely nothing to change Jacob's mind. He was not to seek to cajole him with positive talk or to threaten him with negative talk. God had designs on Jacob, and Laban must keep his hands off.

When Laban finally overtook Jacob, he adhered carefully to what God had said to him. He rebuked Jacob for not allowing him to throw the farewell party (vv. 27-29). He blustered about having the power to do Jacob harm but added quickly that God had warned him about doing so (v. 29). He accused Jacob of stealing his gods (vv. 30-35), an accusation Jacob stoutly denied (without realizing Rachel was in fact the guilty party). But in and through it all, Laban did not seek to persuade Jacob to return. Instead he and Jacob entered into an agreement (vv. 43-55) and went their separate ways with Jacob being glad to be rid of Laban, and Laban at least in some ways being glad to be rid of Jacob.

It was God's protecting and preserving grace that brought all this about. Jacob had trouble resting in this grace. If he had truly been convinced of it, he would not have departed in secret while Laban was far away. Jacob would soon have this trouble again. When he heard that Esau was on his way to meet him with four hundred men, Jacob again doubted God's protecting care (32:6-7). But while God works through our faith, he does not need our faith in order to do his work. His protecting grace was at work even while Jacob was doubting it.

We may also doubt God's protecting grace, but that neither negates nor nullifies it. All the devils of hell will not be able to bring one single child of God to his grave before his appointed time and all the schemes of hell will not be able to keep one child of God out of heaven. God's grace reigns!

While we celebrate the operations of God's grace in this chapter, we must not forget that they took place in the life of a child of God. We have no right to claim these same operations until we have been the recipients of saving grace. Would you like to know if this grace is working in your life? Flee to Jesus Christ as your only hope for salvation. Cast yourself entirely upon him. If you are inclined to do this, you may rest assured God's saving grace is at work. In appealing to you to embrace Christ, I am asking you to resist the way of Laban. Although he knew God's grace was at work in Jacob, he refused to embrace it. He paid lip service to it, but clung to his idols. The grace of God in Christ is the only way of salvation, but merely paying Laban-like lip service to it is not sufficient. We must break with our idols and cling wholeheartedly to Christ.

7.
When Esau comes

Genesis 32:1-21

With his Uncle Laban out of the way, Jacob turned his attention to an even more serious problem — his brother Esau. Jacob knew he could not return to the land of Canaan without sooner or later encountering Esau, who lived in nearby Seir. Deciding sooner was better than later, Jacob sent messengers ahead to beg Esau's favour (vv. 3-5).

Jacob probably felt as if his heart had dropped into his sandals when his messengers returned with these words: 'Esau ... is coming to meet you, and four hundred men are with him' (v. 6).

Jacob was terrified. He had nurtured the hope that Esau would have changed by now, that he no longer desired the death of the brother who had cheated him. But the report sounded as if there had been no change at all, and Jacob found himself face to face with the possibility that he, his family and his servants would soon be departing this life.

This portion of the Word of God speaks to all modern-day saints. Esau and his four hundred men may be taken to represent the problems and fears of life that gallop towards us at breakneck speed. Serious illness, financial hardship, family turmoil, the loss of loved ones are just some of the 'Esaus' we face today.

How are we to cope with such things? Jacob's experience teaches us two mighty strategies for facing the unsettling problems of life.

Trust

First, we must trust the Lord to take care of us in every situation of life. If there was ever a man who had difficulty trusting the Lord, it was Jacob. This is somewhat surprising because of all the reasons he had for trusting. At Bethel the Lord promised to 'keep' him wherever he went and to bring him back to the land of Canaan (28:15). Those promises precluded any possibility that Esau would be able to kill Jacob and his family.

Another reason was that, in his escape from Laban, Jacob was fresh from an experience of the Lord's keeping. Furthermore, the Lord had given Jacob a marvellous indication that his keeping power would continue to be in effect. As Jacob approached the land of Canaan, he was met by 'the angels of God' (v. 1). When Jacob saw these angels, he named the place 'Mahanaim', which means 'two camps' (v. 2).

Commentators are divided on exactly what Jacob had in mind here. Some suggest that the angels of God were themselves divided into two camps, one in front of Jacob and one behind, thus offering him protection all around. Others suggest that Jacob was counting his own entourage as one camp and the angels of God as another camp.

Whichever view we take, Jacob's experience gives us a wonderful insight into what life in this world is like for the saints of God. The angels of God encamp around them.

How we need this word! It is all so very easy for us to fall into the trap of thinking this world is all that there is to reality. The truth is quite different. This world is only half of reality.

The other half is the spiritual world. That world is very real and present, even though it is hidden from our eyes.

A good example of this truth is found in the life of Elisha. When the prophet and his servant found their city surrounded by the Syrians, the servant, stricken with terror, said to Elisha, 'Alas, my master! What shall we do?'

Elisha answered: 'Do not fear, for those who are with us are more than those who are with them.' Then Elisha prayed that the Lord would open the eyes of his servant, and the servant saw 'horses and chariots of fire all around Elisha' (2 Kings 6:15-17).

The saints of God seldom get to see what Jacob and Elisha's servant saw, but all saints should rest in knowing that God's angels are present in this world even when they are not seen, and they are present for the express purpose of ministering to God's people (Heb. 1:14).

It is truly remarkable that Jacob, having seen the angels of God, gave way so soon to doubt and fear, but that is exactly what he did. While surrounded by the countless legions of heaven, Jacob concerned himself with the four hundred men of Esau. Instead of trusting in heaven's resources and in God's promises, Jacob resorted to his own wisdom and relied on his ability to shrewdly manoeuvre circumstances to his advantage. He arranged for a lavish present to be delivered to Esau in stages (vv. 13-21). He then organized his servants and family. His servants, which he valued least, were put first. Then came the less-favoured wife with her children. Then there was the favoured wife, Rachel, and the favoured son, Joseph. Jacob put himself at the back of the procession (vv. 22-24).

All of Jacob's planning and manoeuvring constituted a lack of faith in God. It is easy to see this in Jacob and to condemn it. It is much harder to see and condemn the same in ourselves. Whatever our difficulties and trials, we are called upon to trust the Lord. We would like this to mean that the Lord will very quickly remove the difficulties. But we do not trust the Lord to do what we want done. We rather trust him to do what is best for us. Sometimes God in his wisdom determines that it is best for us to be delivered from our difficulties. Sometimes he determines that it is best for us to face them, just as Jacob had finally to face Esau. Sometimes the Lord determines that it is best to remove us from this world of pain and sorrow to that perfect world where no pain or sorrow can ever touch us again. Whatever God decides for his children, it is for their good and his glory. Let us learn from this, reject the wavering faith of Jacob and trust God.

Pray

The second strategy Jacob teaches us for dealing with the trials of life is to pray. We have found fault with Jacob for his lack of faith. Now we must compliment him for his prayer (vv. 9-12).

Notice to whom it was addressed, that is, to the God of his grandfather Abraham and his father Isaac. Jacob was praying, in the words of A. W. Pink, on 'the ground of a sure and established relationship'.[1]

All children of God can do the same. We can come boldly to God in the hour of our need on the basis of the relationship that has been established with God through the saving work of his Son, Jesus Christ.

Notice, secondly, the appeal to God's promises. Jacob now holds before God the promises that he, God, had given (vv. 9, 12). We have difficulty with this. If God has promised something, why do we need to pray for it at all? The answer is that God delights in hearing his people remind him of the promises that he has made to them. This is, by the way, the basis for confidence in praying. While we may approach God with any desire that is legitimate, we must remind ourselves that he is only obligated to do for us what he has promised. If we can find a promise and cling to it, we know that God will in due time answer our prayer.

Notice also that Jacob prayed with a keen sense of his unworthiness. He says, 'I am not worthy of the least of all the mercies and all the truth which you have shown your servant... ' (v. 10). Concerning this petition, A. W. Pink writes: 'One sometimes wonders if this is the chief reason why so few of us have any real power in prayer today. Certain it is that we must get down into the dust before God if we would receive His blessing. We must come before Him as emptyhanded supplicants, if He is to fill us. We must own our ill deserts, and be ready to receive from Him on the ground of grace alone if we are to have our prayers answered.'[2]

Notice finally that Jacob presented his petition to the Lord, namely, that he be delivered from Esau. It is interesting that Jacob began with God, God's promises and his own unworthiness before ever proceeding to the petition. How often we rush into the presence of God with our petitions without giving thought to any of these other matters! It is no wonder that God is not inclined to answer our prayers.

Jacob's prayer, which can certainly be called a prayer of faith, creates a dilemma for us. It comes between his faithless actions. How could faith and lack of faith exist side by side? How could Jacob move so quickly from lack of faith to faith and back to lack of faith? We can answer this question about Jacob when we are able to answer it about ourselves. Do we not do the same? Do we not sit in church and resolve to live for the Lord only to leave and slide right back into our former way of doing things? Do we not pray earnestly for a closer walk with God only to walk away unchanged? Both Jacob's experience and our own serve to remind us of the reality of the war between the flesh and the spirit. The fact that one is saved does not mean that he no longer has to struggle against the flesh.

It is inevitable that the 'Esaus' of life should come galloping towards us. We cannot avoid them. But we can learn from Jacob on two levels: the negative and the positive. Negatively, we can learn *not to do* as he did and choose rather to trust the Lord to help us in the midst of our evil circumstances. On the positive side, we can learn *to do* as he did, that is, to pray in the midst of such circumstances.

8.
Jacob and the heavenly wrestler

Genesis 32:22-32

Jacob was a man in a dilemma. On one hand, he was about to enter the land of Canaan and realize the promise the Lord had made to him. On the other hand, he was about to encounter his brother Esau who seemed to be set on destroying him and all he possessed.

After making all the necessary preparations he could think of, Jacob was finally alone. Then, suddenly, someone seized him and began to wrestle with him.

Jacob was the man of two unusually powerful and significant experiences. The first of these had occurred twenty years earlier when he was journeying from his home in Canaan to Laban's house. The second now occurs as he is making his journey from Laban's house to Canaan.

There is a lot of debate among Bible students concerning the nature of these two experiences. Some equate the experience at Bethel, in which Jacob saw the ladder extending from earth to heaven, with his conversion. Others think Jacob was not truly converted until this experience of wrestling.

I side with those in the first camp. I believe Jacob was soundly converted to the Lord at Bethel. The very nature of his dream there indicates as much. A ladder was reaching from earth to heaven and God was standing above the ladder.

Heaven was not closed to Jacob. It stood open and it could be entered by means of the ladder. That ladder was none other than a picture of the coming Christ (John 1:51), and I do not doubt that the significance of Jacob's experience at Bethel is that he there looked forward in faith to the coming Messiah.

If Jacob was indeed converted at Bethel, his second glorious experience was of necessity something quite different. How are we to explain this experience? I suggest what we have here is the Lord bringing Jacob to a higher level of spiritual maturity.

It is important to understand that the Lord is at work in this passage. We misread and misuse this passage if we make Jacob the hero of this story, as some do. They focus our attention on Jacob wrestling with God and prevailing. They seem to forget that Jacob wrestled with God only because God first wrestled with him (v. 24). And God wrestled with him in order to move him to a new level of understanding and to a higher level of dependence upon himself.

The truth is that God wrestles with all of his people. He never lets go of those whom he saves. No, he does not wrestle with them in the same way he wrestled with Jacob, but he does wrestle with them in other ways to bring them to the end of themselves and to a more complete reliance upon himself.

The Lord brought Jacob to increased spiritual maturity by making him see three extremely valuable and vital truths.

What really counts in life

First, the Lord showed Jacob what really counts in life. If Jacob had been asked prior to this experience to identify the most important thing in his life, undoubtedly he would have said, 'Esau.' His brother was all he could think about. The clouds in the sky seemed to be stamped with his image. The birds in the trees seemed to sing his name. It had been Esau, Esau, Esau, all day long and into the night.

Jacob was about to learn that he had been mistaken to be so absorbed with Esau. He was suddenly seized by someone who began wrestling with him. It must not have taken long for Jacob to realize that his opponent was no ordinary man. The Lord of heaven was wrestling with him. It was as if the Lord was saying, 'Jacob, instead of worrying about Esau and what he can do, you had better start worrying about me and what I can do.'

We all become twisted in our thinking about what really matters. Those who have never come to faith in Christ are certainly twisted in their thinking. They are consumed and absorbed with this life and give little thought to the God who gives the very air they breathe and who can at any moment stop giving it. They concern themselves exclusively with this world and ignore completely the world to come. Meanwhile Scripture warns constantly about the danger of forgetting eternity (Matt. 16:26; Luke 12:4-5).

Even Christians are not immune from this danger. We have been made citizens of heaven, but we often find ourselves more absorbed with this world and its problems than with God.

Jacob's experience sounds a solemn warning to all. We had better not forget God! He can step in at any time and wrestle with us. He may use serious illness or financial loss or some other kind of severe setback to remind us that he deserves priority.

How to govern life

The Lord's wrestling with Jacob also caused him to see that he had wrongly governed his life up to this point.

Jacob's hip

The Lord drove this message home in two ways. First, he touched Jacob's hip (v. 25). The Bible often speaks of our conduct or manner of life in terms of our 'walk'. There can be no doubt at all about how Jacob had walked prior to this night. He had depended largely upon his own wisdom and strength.

But now, in the course of this wrestling, the Lord touches his hip and Jacob is no longer able to walk as he had before. In other words, in his flesh he was given a reminder of his need to lean always upon God, just as for the rest of his life he had to walk while leaning on a stick.

Jacob's name

The second way in which the Lord drove home Jacob's wrong approach to life was by asking for his name (v. 27). In doing this, the Lord was giving Jacob a painful reminder of his past. The name 'Jacob' meant 'deceiver' or 'supplanter', and Jacob had indeed lived up to his name. By merely saying his own name, Jacob was essentially admitting everything that he had ever been. It had to be a very painful moment indeed for him.

Sufficiency for life

Finally, through the Lord's wrestling with him Jacob was made to see that the Lord was indeed sufficient for him.

When his heavenly visitor made it clear that he had come to wrestle, Jacob may very well have said something like, 'I am in desperate trouble!' But, surprisingly, as the wrestling began, Jacob found himself prevailing. Was this because Jacob was stronger than God? Of course not! The fact that God, with a single touch, dislocated Jacob's hip proved who was stronger. God did not need to wrestle with Jacob at all. One word from him would have been sufficient to reduce Jacob to a pile of ashes. Jacob's success in the wrestling was due, then, to God allowing him to prevail. In doing so the Lord taught Jacob that he, God, could give him the strength for whatever life brought his way.

J. I. Packer writes: 'The nature of Jacob's prevailing with God ... was simply that he had held on to God while God weakened him, and wrought in him the spirit of submission and self-distrust; that he had desired God's blessing so much that he clung to God through all this painful humbling, till he came low enough for God to raise him up by speaking peace to him and assuring him that he need not fear about Esau any more.'[1]

It is quite surprising that Jacob did not mention Esau even once during his wrestling with God. That crisis, which had so dominated his thinking and doing during the day, was now entirely absent. What happened to it? It became lost in something far greater, that is, in Jacob's desire to know God better. Jacob's prayer during his encounter with God was not as he had prayed earlier that day, 'Deliver me ... from the hand of my brother' (v. 11), but rather, 'Tell me your name...' (v. 29).

A person's name represents the person himself. Jacob was pleading, therefore, for the Lord to reveal himself. While the Lord did not answer Jacob's request, he did give him a parting blessing (v. 29).

Our problems and burdens lose their power to overwhelm and crush when we are focusing on God and seeking to know him in a more intimate way. When day finally arrived, Jacob looked back with awe upon what he had experienced. God had graciously come to him and enabled him to prevail. God had blessed him. The name Jacob gave that place, Peniel, expressed his sense of blessing.

And Jacob was no longer the same. Yes, he was still an imperfect man, but now with each limp he is reminded that his strength is not in himself but rather in realizing his weakness and depending completely upon the Lord.

Every child of God moves forward in spiritual understanding and maturity when he realizes the same. Our power lies in our weakness.

9.
Important truths

Genesis 33

This chapter may make us feel that we have descended from a lofty mountain to the lowlands. In the previous chapter, Jacob wrestled with the Lord. In this chapter he meets his brother. This chapter takes us, then, from the glorious and intoxicating to the mundane and unexciting.

While we readily admit this chapter is not exhilarating, we should not sell it short. Embedded in the ore of the mundane are several important truths. This chapter gives us valuable guidelines for governing our own lives. None of us will ever have the experience Jacob had in chapter 32, but, if we hope to live well, we will certainly need to master the truths that emerge from his experiences in chapter 33.

The importance of trusting the Lord

After his experience of wrestling with the Lord, Jacob went out to meet his brother (v. 3). The day before, Jacob had made sure that his company was arranged so that he was last (32:22-23), but now he is in the forefront. James Montgomery Boice observes: 'But after wrestling with the angel and being subdued by him, Jacob received new courage and actually preceded his household when the meeting took place. Having been conquered by God, Jacob became strong and went forward in the might of the one who had conquered him.'[1]

The thing that leaps out at us from this account is the changed attitude of Esau. His pledge to kill his brother was now completely forgotten. When Esau saw Jacob he 'ran to meet him, and embraced him, and fell on his neck and kissed him, and they wept' (v. 4).

How are we to explain the change in Esau? Many would be inclined to attribute it to the passing of time. While there is truth in the adage 'Time heals all wounds', we must not be satisfied with that as the sole explanation. The Christian cannot help but see God's hand in everything. We remind ourselves that God was at work in Jacob's life in a special way. God had designs on this man. He was intent on bringing him back to the land of Canaan and achieving in Jacob what he, the Lord, had purposed. The Lord was not about to let Esau frustrate or thwart his purpose. So he gave Esau a different attitude. The book of Proverbs says:

> When a man's ways please the LORD,
> He makes even his enemies
>   to be at peace with him

> (Prov. 16:7).

A. W. Pink writes perceptively: 'Jacob had devoted much thought to the problem how *he* could best propitiate the brother whose anger he feared, and had gone to much expense and trouble to this end. But it accomplished nothing! It was all labor lost as the sequel shows. *God* had "appeased" Esau, just as before *He* had quietened Laban! How much better then had Jacob just been "still" and trusted in the Lord to act for him.'[2]

There is a lesson for us in all this. The same God who changed Esau still changes hearts today. Let us never give up on anyone!

The importance of reconciliation

This chapter also speaks powerfully to us about the importance of reconciling with those with whom we have been at odds.

This was a meeting that the Lord would not allow Jacob to dodge or postpone. The Lord had laid hold of him and moved him to a higher level of spirituality and devotion than he had occupied before. Jacob was now Israel, and he must act like Israel. He could not walk with the Lord as Israel and ignore the damage he had done as Jacob.

Through his encounter with the Lord, Jacob now found himself gripped by the principle that his grandfather had stated to his nephew Lot: 'Please let there be no strife between you and me ... for we are brethren' (Gen. 13:8).

How we need to learn from this episode! Untold damage is being done to the cause of Christ by Christians who are at odds with one another. Sometimes friction is created by real offences; but all too often it springs from things that are incredibly trivial. Whatever the cause of the friction, those of us who know the Lord are under his command to forgive from the heart those who have trespassed against us.

This does not mean we have to go back and rehash the problem. That may just give it new life! It is interesting that neither Jacob nor Esau mentioned what had transpired between them years before. Both men were content to let the past be the past. Let us learn from them!

The importance of obedience

A third truth this chapter lays before us is the importance of obedience to the Lord. After taking his leave of Esau, Jacob 'journeyed to Succoth, built himself a house, and made booths for his livestock' (v. 17). After dwelling there for a while, he finally entered the land of Canaan by going to Shechem (v. 18).

There is considerable debate among commentators on whether Jacob was right to tarry at Succoth and then go on to Shechem. It appears that he was disobedient to the Lord in going to each of these sites. The Lord had clearly commanded him to return to Canaan (31:3), and Succoth was not in the land.

Jacob's own words to his wives while they were still at Laban's house would seem to indicate that the Lord had specifically commanded him to return to Bethel (31:13). If so, Jacob was wrong to go to Shechem. The tragic incident that occurred there (34:1-31) would appear to verify that Jacob went there in disobedience.

If Jacob was disobedient in going to these sites, it serves as a powerful reminder to us of the truth that the child of God is not perfect even though he has been changed by the grace of God.

It is noteworthy that although Jacob's name had been changed to Israel (32:28), Scripture subsequently uses the name Jacob twice as often as it uses Israel. On the other hand, when Abram's name was changed to Abraham, the latter was used consistently from then on.[3]

All of this gives evidence of a fierce struggle in Jacob between the flesh and the spirit, a struggle that is present in every saint of God. Because this struggle is so real and painful, we must constantly heed the words of the apostle Paul:

'Walk in the Spirit, and you shall not fulfil the lust of the flesh. For the flesh lusts against the Spirit, and the Spirit against the flesh...' (Gal. 5:16-17).

Some would offer us a brand of spirituality that lifts us above all struggle and conflict in this life. But the Bible offers us an armour that must be donned every day because the battle against the world, the flesh and the devil rages every day (Eph. 6:10-20).

Communion with the Lord

Finally, this chapter shows us the importance of communion with the Lord. While Jacob was encamped at Shechem, he built an altar to the Lord (v. 20). How cheering is the truth this presents us! The fact that a child of God strays into disobedience does not mean that there are absolutely no evidences at all of spiritual life in him. The grace of God that creates faith in the believer nurtures and sustains that faith. Even in the midst of disobedience, grace sees to it that the believer will never completely fall away from his faith. It guarantees that the saint will be miserable in his sins and will still know a yearning for God. Falling into sin cannot displace or dislodge that grace.

> Grace taught my soul to pray,
> And pardoning love to know;
> 'Twas grace that kept me to this day,
> And will not let me go.[4]
>
> Philip Doddridge (1702-51)

This thirty-third chapter of Genesis is, then, something of a mixed bag. On the positive side, Jacob reconciles with Esau and builds an altar. On the negative side, he disobeys the commands of the Lord about his journey. In the light of these things we might say that Jacob was learning to limp. His limp was the reminder in his flesh that he was to conduct his life with a keen awareness that he must no longer trust in himself and his wisdom but rather in the Lord. Sometimes Jacob succeeded and sometimes he failed. But the grace of the Lord that had changed him was there all along — even when he failed.

That same grace is at work in all the people of God. It has made us the children of God. It pardons us when we fail. And it will finally lead us home.

10.
An ugly and sordid episode

Genesis 34

Here we have one of the ugliest incidents in the Bible. Jacob's daughter Dinah is raped by the Shechemites, and the Shechemites are killed by Jacob's vengeful sons.

It is a chapter that most pastors ignore, undoubtedly agreeing with H. C. Leupold: 'We may well wonder if any man who had proper discernment ever drew a text from this chapter.'[1] What possible justification is there for us giving attention to a chapter that is generally considered 'off-limits'? The answer is quite simple: it is in the Bible. And all the Bible is, according to the apostle Paul, profitable for us (2 Tim. 3:16). That includes this unpleasant episode before us.

What, then, are we to learn from this chapter? While it yields several important truths, we will restrict ourselves to four.

The nature of the Bible

The first has to do with the nature of the Bible. Here we are dealing with the life of Jacob. This man certainly has to be considered one of the greatest in the Bible. He had indescribably glorious spiritual experiences, and yet we find him involved in this sordid episode.

Now if the Bible were a mere human book, no doubt this sad affair would have been excluded. But the Bible never sweeps under the carpet the follies and failures of its heroes. It rather sets them in the clear light of day that we might profit from them. It tells us of Noah's drunkenness, Abraham's lapses of faith, Moses' anger, David's adultery, Solomon's idolatries and Simon Peter's denials of Jesus.

All of these remarkable accounts constitute firm evidence that the Bible is exactly what it claims to be: the infallible Word of God.

The sinfulness of human nature

This chapter also confirms for us what the Bible says about the sinfulness of human nature. What a revolting list of sins we have here! Here is lust and rape (v. 2). Here is deception (v. 13). Here is murder (v. 25). Here is plundering (vv. 27-28). And, yes, we even have here the sad spectacle of men using religion for evil purposes. The sons of Jacob used the religious rite of circumcision to set the stage for their brutal slaying of the Shechemites (vv. 13-26).

The Bible insists that such unsavoury actions flow from a heart that is diseased and defiled by sin (Matt. 12:35; 15:18-20). A casual study of what the Bible says about human nature leads us to conclude that we are totally depraved. That does not mean we are as bad as we can possibly be. It rather means that every part of us is touched and tainted by sin, and sin can and does break out in our actions in very surprising and disgusting ways.

While we may feel like congratulating ourselves on not doing the things we find recorded in this chapter, we must recognize that we are capable of doing very wicked things indeed because we carry within us the seeds of every type of wickedness. We may not commit the act of murder, but if we have hatred in our hearts we have committed murder. We may not commit the act of adultery, but if we have lust in our hearts, we are guilty of adultery (Matt. 5:21-30).

The reality of backsliding

This incident also shows us how terribly low a child of God can sink. We cannot say with certainty how many of Jacob's sons had come to true faith in God. We must always remember that God's covenant with Jacob's family did not mean that his sons were automatically children of God. Each member of the covenant family still had to embrace that covenant in faith.

It is impossible for us to say how many of Jacob's sons, if any, had done so at this particular time. But we do know that Jacob was a true child of God, and we would like to be able to say that he functions in this chapter as a man of faith; but the facts will not allow us to do so.

The very fact that Jacob and his family were living in the area of Shechem is a testimony to his failure to live in complete obedience to God. God had clearly told him to go to Bethel (31:13), but instead Jacob had settled at Succoth and Shechem.

The Bible is full of examples of children of God being in the wrong place: Lot in Sodom, Elijah under the broom tree, Jonah in the hold of a boat headed for Tarshish, David on the rooftop gazing at Bathsheba; all are powerful reminders of how important it is for God's people to stay away from places where they do not belong and of the terrible damage they create when they fail to do so.

Are you today, child of God, where you ought to be? Or are you in the wrong place? Are you spending a lot of time with people who have no regard for the laws of God and who are likely to bring you to harm? Are you going to places where temptation so abounds that it is almost impossible to resist it?

We must also fault Jacob for failing to offer decisive leadership in this situation. After Dinah was raped, the perpetrator and his father came to Jacob to propose marriage and an arrangement that would allow their peoples to intermarry (vv. 8-12).

Jacob fumbled badly at this point. He seems to have been utterly indecisive. It is striking that he quickly fades out of the picture and his sons come to the forefront. In fact there is no mention of Jacob at all from verses 7 to 29, but the phrase 'the sons of Jacob' appears four times (vv. 7, 13, 25, 27). Only after his sons had exacted their bloody revenge on the Shechemites does Jacob finally re-enter the picture (v. 30).

This is hardly how we would expect the head of God's covenant family to act! A far more fitting response would have been for him to have called his family together, confessed that the tragic rape of Dinah was due to his own failure to obey God and moved his family immediately to Bethel.

Jacob's failure in this situation reminds us once again that the children of God are not perfect in this life.

The stubborn grace of God

Most of the truths upon which we have fastened are very sobering and even depressing. But there is yet another truth that emerges from the sordid details of this chapter, namely, the stubborn grace of God.

We look in vain for any mention of God in this chapter. The Shechemites are here. Jacob and his sons are here. But God is absent.

The fact that God is not mentioned does not mean, of course, that he was unaware of all these developments. God ever watches over human events. Nothing is hidden from his eyes. The Lord saw it all. He saw the wickedness that Shechem perpetrated against Dinah, the weakness of Jacob in dealing with the situation and the wicked plotting and actions of Jacob's sons. And he sees our wickedness as well. We may think he is busy elsewhere or that our sins are tucked away so securely that he is not aware of them, but such thoughts are dreadfully mistaken. Nothing escapes God.

We might think, in light of the abounding and sickening wickedness of this chapter, that the Lord would wash his hands of Jacob and his family, that he would simply walk away and leave them to their wickedness and its consequences. But the next chapter begins with these blessed words: 'Then God said to Jacob'.

As we survey chapter 35, we find God is very prominent again. Note these phrases: 'Then God appeared' (v. 9), 'And God said' (v. 10), 'Also God said' (v. 11), and 'Then God went up' (v. 13).

All of this leads us to a cheering and happy conclusion: God never lets his people go. His grace is greater than their sin! He is the God who, centuries later, would not let his servant David go. Even though David committed terrible sins, the Lord would not let him go. He is the God who would forgive and restore Simon Peter after the latter had denied the Lord Jesus Christ three times.

He is the God who is so wonderfully pictured in Jesus' parable of the prodigal son. He is ever the father who is ready to receive his wayward children and to restore them to full fellowship with himself.

Have you, child of God, strayed far from the Lord? Have you been living at Shechem, the place of broken vows, broken hearts and broken lives? No matter how far you have strayed, there is forgiveness with the Lord. Turn from your sin and seek him today.

11.
Back to Bethel:
God's renewing grace

Genesis 35

The opening words of this chapter are astonishing and incredibly wonderful: 'Then God said to Jacob, "Arise, go up to Bethel ... and make an altar there to God..."'

What grace is this! God speaks to Jacob and calls him to spiritual renewal even though Jacob and his family had strayed so very far from him. Shechem was the place of backsliding and all its wretched results. It was the place of broken hearts and shattered lives. But here the Lord calls Jacob to Bethel, the place of God's presence and blessing.

How we need this chapter! The sad truth is that many of God's people are living at Shechem today. They are far from the Lord, but he refuses to let them go. He ever calls his people to Bethel.

The crucial question for all straying saints may be put in this way: how do we get back to Bethel? In other words, how do we return to the place of spiritual vitality? This passage supplies us with some answers.

Revisiting salvation

We must first say that we can only return to spiritual vitality by remembering or revisiting our salvation. We must remember that the Lord first made himself known to Jacob at Bethel (Gen. 28:10-22). The Lord's command to Jacob to return there was, then, equivalent to asking him to recall what had taken place there years before. How long has it been, child of God, since you revisited your salvation? We need to do this often. Nothing so warms the heart and rekindles the fire of devotion.

The church of Ephesus gives us an example of this very thing. This church was sound in doctrine, holy in life and energetic in service, but the Lord Jesus Christ was still not pleased with them because they had allowed the flame of their love for him to burn low. What was the antidote for this church? The Lord Jesus put it in these words: 'Remember therefore from where you have fallen; repent and do the first works...' (Rev. 2:5).

Spiritual renewal would begin for this church through remembering. What were they to remember? Their first love. And what is their first love? It is the love that Christians have for the Lord when they first come to know him.

You remember that love. You remember being amazed that the Lord Jesus had saved one as unworthy and undeserving as yourself. You remember the profound relief that you felt over your condemnation being lifted and your sins being forgiven. You remember your astonishment that you had been adopted into God's family and given eternal life. You remember thinking that there was nothing you would not be willing to do for your glorious Saviour, Jesus Christ. You remember thinking that nothing could ever cause your love for Christ to flag or falter.

But every child of God has to admit that at one time or another his love has faltered. The lure of the world, the lusts of the flesh, the wiles of the devil, the burdens and hardships of life, the discouragement of seeing few results from our efforts; all of these things and others have a way of diminishing our love for the Lord and our zeal for his cause.

But our first love can be renewed and restored. Think of the depth of your sin. Think of the eternal destruction that was looming before you. Think of the Lord Jesus Christ, who did not have to do anything for you, coming to this world and taking upon himself the penalty for your sins. Yes, remember; and in remembering you will find your heart drawn back to the Saviour.

Breaking with idols

Returning to spiritual vitality also requires us to break with our idols. Jacob responded to the Lord's command to return to Bethel in this way: 'Put away the foreign gods that are among you... ' (v. 2).

What a shocking thing for him to say! No, it was not shocking that Jacob would command his family to put away their gods. It is shocking that they had such gods to put away. This was the covenant family, the family through which God would fulfil his promise of the Messiah. This was supposed to be the family of faith in God and in his promises. And yet they had their idols and had evidently possessed them for a long while (Gen. 31:26-35).

Now God was calling them to spiritual renewal, and Jacob understood that such renewal was impossible apart from the destruction of those idols. Bethel cannot coexist with idols.

We do not have the little household images that Jacob's family possessed, but we do have our idols. Anything that receives from us the allegiance and devotion that belong to God alone is an idol, whether it be money, pleasure, career, sports or even family.

The family of Jacob complied with his request by bringing their idols to him, which he then buried under a tree (v. 4).

Do we desire a closeness to God? Do we long for genuine revival? Are we willing to get the shovel out and bury our idols; and leave them buried?

Communing with the Lord

Returning to spiritual vitality also requires us to commune with the Lord. When Jacob arrived in Bethel he 'built an altar there' (v. 7). The altar represents communion and prayer.

Prayer is always the indispensable means of renewal. The prophet Hosea made this point forcefully with the people of his generation:

> O Israel, return to the LORD your God,
> For you have stumbled because of your iniquity;
> Take words with you,
> And return to the LORD.
> Say to him,
> 'Take away all iniquity;
> Receive us graciously,
> For we will offer the sacrifices of our lips'
>
> (Hos. 14:1-2).

How were the people to return to the Lord? They were to do so by taking words with them; in other words, they were to pray. They were to confess their sins and cast themselves upon the mercy of the Lord. Jacob found renewal in this way, and the people of Hosea's time could have found it as well, but they refused to heed his words and brought severe calamity upon themselves.

Occupying ourselves with God

Finally, returning to spiritual vitality requires us to occupy ourselves with God. This passage includes a little note that at first seems to be rather insignificant. It tells us that Jacob changed the name of Bethel to El Bethel. The former means 'House of God', while the latter means 'The God of the House of God'. This would seem to suggest that Jacob had truly sought the Lord and the Lord had become very real to him.

Jacob's experience at this point speaks very pointedly to us about a terrible danger. If we are not careful we can become more concerned about the benefits revival produces than we are about the God who produces those benefits. In other words, we can become more concerned about God's gifts than we are about him, the giver.

God wants us to seek him just because we love him and desire him and not because of what we can get from him. We parents would be highly offended if we sensed that our children were more interested in what they can get from us than they are in us. It is no different with God.

A good example of focusing on God rather than on what he gives comes from an episode in the life of Simon Peter. After he and others had fished all night without success, the Lord Jesus commanded them to let down their nets for a catch. These men expected nothing, but they were in for a shock. Their nets were filled with fish! Simon Peter, however, did not focus on the fish. Instead he focused on the Lord who had provided the fish and said, 'Depart from me, for I am a sinful man, O Lord!' (Luke 5:8).

If we want to return to the spiritual vitality of Bethel, we must do as Jacob and Simon Peter did — focus on the Lord simply because he is the Lord and is worthy of our adoration and devotion.

Jacob did indeed receive wonderful benefits from going back to Bethel. He and his family received the Lord's protection from those who would do them harm (v. 5). He received a reaffirmation of the Lord's covenant with him (vv. 9-15). But Jacob received these things while occupying himself with God. We do indeed receive benefits from doing just that, but the main benefit of occupying ourselves with God is God himself. May he help us to hunger and thirst for him!

12.
The sorrows of Jacob

Genesis 35:16-22; 37:31-35; 38:1-30;
42:36-38; 43:1-14; 45:9, 25-28

With the sole exception of Job, no one in the Old Testament experienced more sorrow than Jacob. We find him encountering many sorrows before we come to the above passages. We remember the conflict and turmoil he experienced while he was still at home with his parents and his brother. We remember the trouble he experienced during the twenty years he stayed with his Uncle Laban. Specifically, there were during that time four major heartaches: receiving Leah as his wife when he expected to wed Rachel; having to work seven extra years for Rachel; the barrenness of Rachel; and the unhappiness of his dealings with Laban.

After he left Laban's house, Jacob experienced yet another sorrow, that of seeing his sons take unnecessary vengeance on the Shechemites (34:1-31).

Heaped upon all these sorrows are those conveyed in the verses noted above: the death of Rachel as she was giving birth to another son (35:16-20); the flagrant immorality of two sons, Reuben (35:21-22) and Judah (38:1-30); the presumed death of Joseph (37:31-35); and the fear of losing yet another son, Benjamin (42:36-38).

It is obvious that Jacob walked many a mile with sorrow. She often accompanied him to his bed. She frequently set his table and dined with him. She went with him to his tasks and greeted him when he came home.

Many people of faith have no trouble identifying with Jacob at this point. They know about sorrow. She has often been their companion as well. And when they come across a sorrowing saint in the Word of God, they find themselves eagerly scanning the biblical record for lessons and insights from which they themselves can draw.

What does the account of Jacob have to say to sorrowing saints?

We are not exempt from sorrow

First, it tells us that the people of God are not exempt from sorrow in this life. Some would have us believe that saints can slide through life without having to experience hardship and difficulty. They contend that it is God's purpose and design for each of his children to be unfailingly healthy, fabulously wealthy and continuously happy. If a child of God finds himself treading on a lower plane, he is living beneath what God intends for him. If he would only have enough faith, all his problems would vanish and he would enjoy uninterrupted victory.

Many hold the belief that one can have a spiritual experience of such magnitude that it precludes sorrows and difficulties for ever. But look at Jacob. He had three first-rate experiences of the presence and glory of God (28:10-22; 32:22-32; 35:1-15). These were of a far higher calibre than we will ever know. But Jacob went from such heights to the sorrows mentioned in our texts. The spiritual experiences did not lift him above difficulty and hardship for ever.

The same truth is presented again and again in Scripture. Paul lived as close to God as anyone, and yet he knew many sorrows (2 Cor. 11:22-33). The Lord Jesus himself plainly said to his disciples, 'In the world you will have tribulation...' (John 16:33).

We must not invite sorrow

A second lesson we can draw from Jacob is to be careful that we do not bring sorrows upon ourselves. As we re-examine the list of Jacob's sorrows, we see that they fall into two categories. The death of Rachel cannot be attributed to any failure on Jacob's part, but we cannot help but think that his other sorrows flowed to some extent from his own failings.

While we certainly do not absolve Reuben and Judah of their immorality, we must acknowledge the poor example Jacob set by marrying two wives and fathering children through two concubines. While we do not absolve the eleven sons of Jacob for their treatment of Joseph, we must consider the jealousy Jacob fostered by showing favouritism to Joseph.

Behind these specific examples, we have to note the shocking lack of faith in Jacob's family. We must never forget that this was the covenant family. God had made himself known to them. He had made stunningly glorious promises to them. The flame of faith should have been burning brightly in Jacob's sons but it often appeared to be barely flickering. A long association with the Canaanites had apparently caused these men to become just like them.

We must also never forget that the hatred of these men for their brother Joseph was not due entirely to the favourit-ism shown by their father. A large proportion was due to the fact that God had selected Joseph to speak his Word to them. Joseph was a living rebuke to them and their ways.

Even Jacob himself often seems to be deficient in faith. These chapters that document his sorrows have nothing to say about his faith. We might say God is conspicuous by his absence. The most shocking example of the low state of Jacob's faith is found in his response to Joseph's dreams. Having himself heard from God through this medium (28:10-12), Jacob should have discerned that God was speaking through Joseph and responded more positively (37:9-11).

All of this tells us not to invite sorrows into our lives. There will be enough sorrow in life without creating any more. How many of our sorrows are self-inflicted by refusing to trust and obey God!

We must rest in God's purpose

A third lesson we learn from Jacob's sorrows is that God always has a purpose in the sorrows of his children. We all have a tendency to interpret God's dealings with us in very individualistic terms. If a particular circumstance makes us happy, we are inclined to conclude that God is doing his job well. If a circumstance makes us unhappy, we might allow ourselves to think he has failed.

One of the hardest lessons for us to learn is that God has purposes that are far greater than ourselves. He does not exist to make each individual as happy as he or she can possibly be. God's purpose is to carry out his plan of redemption and to do so in a way that will bring glory to himself and bring all his people to glory.

Why was it necessary for Joseph to be sold into slavery in Egypt and for Jacob to spend years thinking he was dead? It seems cruel if we think only in terms of Jacob alone. But when we step back and look at the bigger picture, we see that God brought sorrow to Jacob so that he could bring happiness to untold numbers. By putting Joseph in Egypt, God paved the way for all Jacob's family to settle in a place where they could grow into a nation without any danger of them being absorbed into Canaanite culture.

No one stated it better than Joseph himself. The years had come and gone. Jacob was now dead, and Joseph's brothers were afraid that he, Joseph, might now exact revenge on them for selling him into slavery. But Joseph allayed their fears with these words: 'But as for you, you meant evil against me; but God meant it for good, in order to bring it about as it is this day, to save many people alive' (Gen. 50:20).

We cannot think of Jacob enduring sorrow for the sake of many without thinking of the Lord Jesus Christ. Oh, what sorrows he endured in his public ministry, in the shadows of Gethsemane and on the cross of Calvary! Why was it necessary for him to endure such sorrow? The answer is the same as in Jacob's case. Jesus had to endure sorrow so that God could bring happiness to countless multitudes. Jesus had to endure sorrow so that his people could enjoy forgiveness of sins and eternal life.

True faith rallies in the midst of sorrows

Let us note one more of the many lessons we can learn here, that is, that true faith will always rally in the midst of sorrows.

We have noticed that Jacob's faith was often weak. Every child of God knows that faith does not always shine brightly. Sometimes it goes through an eclipse. But faith is a stubborn grace. When Satan thinks he has stamped it out, its dying embers take flame again. Faith always rallies. Sorrow cannot destroy it.

We find one such rally when Jacob was faced with the decision of whether to allow his sons to take his youngest son Benjamin to Egypt. The famine was severe in Canaan, and there was food in Egypt. But the ruler of Egypt, whom we know was Joseph, had inexplicably demanded that the sons of Jacob should not return without their younger brother. Jacob was sure that he would lose Benjamin if he acquiesced to this demand. But then faith took hold, and Jacob decided to send Benjamin, saying as he did so, 'And may God Almighty give you mercy before the man... ' (Gen. 43:14).

The difficulties of life may mount up all around us. Sorrow may gather like thunderclouds over our heads. But faith will never allow the children of God to forget that their God is mighty to sustain them in the midst of the sorrows and to finally deliver them from all their grief.

13.

A message too good to be true and the carts of Egypt

Genesis 45:21-28

A trip to Egypt in Jacob's time was no small undertaking. It was a matter of several weeks. The weeks involved in his sons' second trip to Egypt to buy food had to rank as some of the most difficult of Jacob's life. He had reluctantly allowed his youngest son Benjamin to go along. The mysterious ruler in Egypt had made it clear that he would not sell them any more food unless they brought their youngest brother with them (Gen. 42:20).

During those anxious weeks, Jacob often must have felt despair. Would he ever again see Benjamin, the only remaining son from his beloved Rachel? Would he ever see any of his sons again? As the weeks dragged along, he often lifted yearning eyes to scan the horizon for the sight of his sons.

Then one day the waiting ended. There on the horizon was a caravan. As the figures drew closer, Jacob was flooded with relief. His sons, including Benjamin, had returned. Jacob thought he could never be happier than he was at that moment. He was about to find that he could. When they saw him, his sons may very well have begun to run, shouting excitedly that Joseph was still alive and was governor of Egypt (v. 26).

This was impossible. The report had to be mistaken. His son had been dead for years. This was news too good to be true. The account says that Jacob 'did not believe them' (v. 26).

That was his initial response; but it soon changed. In a matter of moments, he moved from unbelief to faith. The account closes with these words: 'Then Israel said, "It is enough. Joseph my son is still alive. I will go and see him before I die"' (v. 28).

This passage should be of vital interest to us. It has to do with each and every one of us because we either are or have been in exactly the same position as Jacob when he heard the news about Joseph.

The Bible claims to have a message for each of us without exception. It is a message that in many ways seems too good to be true. It begins by telling us that we are all by nature sinners and under the wrath of God who is holy. But it proceeds to tell us that our sins can be forgiven. It tells us that God can and will declare us guiltless, that he will adopt us into his own family. Furthermore, it tells us that when we die he will receive our souls into his presence, he will eventually raise our bodies from the grave and we will live with him in glory for ever.

The most astonishing thing about all of this is that God bestows all these unspeakable benefits upon us on the basis of his Son coming into this world in the form of a man and dying on a Roman cross. It tells us that this crucified Jesus is now ruler in heaven just as Joseph was in Egypt. Furthermore, it tells us that Christ's kingship will be acknowledged universally one day.

All of this constitutes a message that appears too good to be true, a message that cannot and should not be believed. And many do not hesitate to say that they would like to believe it, but they find it quite impossible to do so.

My purpose is to move each one who has rejected this message to embrace it here and now. I would, by the grace and power of God, move each unbeliever to follow Jacob in his journey from unbelief to belief, by asking you to consider the very things that convinced him of the truth of the message he received about Joseph.

The testimony of eyewitnesses

First, Jacob was convinced by the testimony of eyewitnesses. At first he rejected the message of his sons while being in a completely inferior position. They had been to Egypt. They had seen and heard things there that convinced them. But here was Jacob, who had not been to Egypt, deciding that their report was unreliable.

It did not take him long to realize his inferior position. His sons were standing before him, talking about what they had seen and heard. Jacob knew them. They had become reliable, trustworthy men. They had no reason to lie. They all said the same thing. As he pondered these things, his unbelief began to melt away and faith began to pour in.

This part of Jacob's pilgrimage from unbelief to faith speaks powerfully to all who have not received Christ. The Bible's message about the Lord Jesus is credible and trustworthy. It was penned by men who associated with him and observed him very carefully. Here is the testimony of one of those men, John: 'That which was from the beginning, which we have heard, which we have seen with our eyes, which we have looked upon, and our hands have handled, concerning the Word of life ... that which we have seen and heard we declare to you, that you also may have fellowship with us; and truly our fellowship is with the Father and with his Son Jesus Christ' (1 John 1:1, 3).

When Luke began writing the Gospel that bears his name, he wanted the one to whom he wrote, Theophilus, to understand that his Gospel was based on eyewitness accounts of what Jesus said and did (Luke 1:1-3). In other words, Luke wanted Theophilus to have certainty regarding Jesus Christ (Luke 1:4).

We cannot speak to the eyewitnesses of Jesus' mighty deeds. But we have their account in Scripture, which we do well to heed.

The nature of the report

In the second place, Jacob was convinced by the nature of what was reported to him. Verse 27 says his sons reported to him 'all the words which Joseph had said to them'. We have at least some of those words (45:3-13). As we examine them, we find that they include several references to God (vv. 5, 7, 8, 9). It was always 'God, God, God' with Joseph, and we have no trouble at all imagining Jacob saying, 'That sounds just like Joseph!' as he heard his sons' report.

Many can testify to something very similar to Jacob's experience. As they read what the Bible has to say about the reality and the depth of human sin, the certainty of God's judgement and the nature of the salvation God has provided, they found themselves hearing 'the ring of truth'. In other words, they found the message making sense. They found themselves saying, 'Yes, of course. How could it be any other way?'

The Bible carries this ring of truth about it. There is a sense in which it carries its own authentication with it. Its words are divine in origin and in nature, and merely reading them often creates the conviction that they are true.

Do you, unbelieving friend, hear the ring of truth in Scripture today? If you do, God is working in you to move you to faith. Yield to his working power and receive his salvation.

The indisputable proofs

The final and decisive factor in Jacob coming to embrace the report of his sons was what we may call indisputable proofs of the veracity of his sons' message. Our passage sets this out in these words: '...when he saw the carts which Joseph had sent to carry him, the spirit of Jacob their father revived' (v. 27).

The carts of Egypt spoke volumes to Jacob. His sons did not have those carts when they undertook the journey to Egypt. How did they come to have them? They had clearly received them while they were in Egypt. Those carts were visible proofs.

Here we are confronted with the message of the Bible, a message that often appears, as we have noted, too good to be true. Is this message backed up by any kind of evidence? Yes, it purports to be the message of eyewitnesses, but does it have any corroborating evidence? Yes, it rings true, but is there any substantiation beyond that?

There are, I suggest, some proofs that are just as powerful for us as the carts of Egypt were for Jacob. The resurrection of Jesus is one such proof. This was one of the best substantiated events in all of history. The tomb was empty. The disciples were changed. Over five hundred people saw the risen Christ (1 Cor. 15:6). If Christ arose from the dead, he is obviously no mere man but is in fact exactly what the Bible claims, and the Bible is corroborated.

The fulfilled prophecies of Scripture constitute another such proof. Someone has counted 325 instances of fulfilled prophecy in the Bible. Each fulfilled prophecy proves that the Bible is a divine book and its message is true and reliable.

The archaeological discoveries are yet another of these proofs. There has never been an instance of archaeology disproving some detail in the Word of God, but there are numerous instances where it confirms such details. Each of these confirmations indicates that the Bible's message is indeed true and can be trusted.

I appeal to all who think this message is too good to be true to receive it. It comes to us on good authority. It carries the ring of truth. It is confirmed by indisputable evidences. Those who heed this message will not find that it is too good to be true. They will simply find that it is true, and they will bless the grace of God that enabled them to believe it.

14.
Sweet consolations for the challenges of life

Genesis 46:1-7

When he learned that Joseph was still alive, Jacob was thrilled beyond measure. As the sense of exhilaration faded, Jacob found himself facing a sobering reality. Joseph wanted him to come to Egypt, not just to visit but to settle (45:9-11).

This would constitute a major change for Jacob. He was old. Egypt was very different, and perhaps dangerous. And Canaan was both his home and the land God had promised to give his descendants. These circumstances made Joseph's proposal appear problematic, to say the least. There certainly was nothing wrong with a visit, but was it God's will for him to settle there?

Jacob had determined that he would know the Lord's will about the matter before he left the land of Canaan. He began his journey to Egypt and paused at Beersheba, which was at the very border of the land of Canaan. Beersheba was exceedingly rich in spiritual significance. Jacob's grandfather Abraham had called on the Lord there (21:33), and it was where his father Isaac had received confirmation of the Lord's covenant with Abraham (26:23-25). There at Beersheba, while he was engaged in worship, Jacob received the help he needed. There the Lord spoke to him. How often God speaks to his people when they come to him in worship! How often life's problems melt away in the warm glow of heartfelt adoration of God!

God's personal interest and care

How did the Lord's words help Jacob? They first reminded him of God's personal interest and care.

The Lord began his message by calling 'Jacob, Jacob!' (v. 2). The Lord knew all about Jacob. He knew where he was and what was troubling him. Many years prior to this, the Lord had given Jacob the name 'Israel', which means 'prince with God' (32:28). We cannot help but wonder if the Lord here used the name 'Jacob' as a gentle rebuke to the patriarch for allowing himself to be filled with anxiety about the future.

In one sense, we are not at all like Jacob. He occupied a unique place in the economy of God. But in another way, we are very much like him. We often find ourselves perplexed and anxious about our circumstances, quick to tremble and slow to trust. Let us take consolation from Jacob's experience. As the Lord knew his name and his circumstances, so he knows ours. And he feels the same tender concern for us that he felt for Jacob.

It may often seem that we are not at all important to God; that we are surrounded with enormous trials and difficulties and he takes no notice of us. No less an authority than the Lord Jesus Christ himself assures us that this feeling is not well founded. Our Father in heaven has such an eye for detail that he marks the sparrow's fall. And we are far more important to him than sparrows. He has the very hairs of our heads numbered, and we can be assured that he is concerned about everything that grieves and troubles us (Matt. 6:25-34). How blessed we are to have such a God!

God's perfect faithfulness

The Lord's words also helped Jacob by reminding him of God's perfect faithfulness. After calling Jacob's name, the Lord said, 'I am God, the God of your father...' (v. 3).

It would have been marvellous enough if God had merely said, 'I am God.' By the way, the God of the Bible is the only one who can truly say this. There are plenty of false gods around, but there is only one true God.

If God had added nothing, Jacob would have had cause to rejoice. He could have said, 'What a wonder! The only living and true God has spoken to me and called me by name.'

But God also reminded Jacob that he was the God of his father. This brought to Jacob's mind that he and his family were in a special covenant relationship with God. God was the God of Jacob's father Isaac because he had also been the God of Isaac's father Abraham. God had called Abraham out of idolatry and had given him astonishing promises. He, Abraham, would be the father of a new nation into which the Lord Jesus Christ would be born. Abraham would also be the father of a spiritual nation consisting of all those who would put their faith in Christ.

Jacob was part of the covenant the Lord had established with his grandfather Abraham, and that covenant was still in effect. Jacob was a very flawed man in many ways, but his failures could not negate that covenant. It rested, not on Jacob himself, but rather on God who is always faithful to his promises. Every believer in Jesus Christ has entered into this covenant. Through Christ we have forgiveness of sins and eternal life. In the final analysis, it does not matter what happens to us in this life. God's covenant precludes any possibility of any real harm coming to us.

We may also assume that the phrase 'the God of your father' caused Jacob to bring to mind the many trials and tribulations his father had experienced. As he thought about these, Jacob came to realize that God had seen his father through much. As Jacob pondered this, he was forced to conclude that the God who had guided and sustained his father would surely guide and sustain him — even in Egypt!

God's encouraging promises

Finally, the Lord's words helped Jacob in that they included encouraging promises. Verses 3 and 4 include four promises.

A great nation

First, the Lord promised to make a great nation of Jacob's descendants while they were in Egypt. Jacob's settling in Egypt was God's purpose. If he had stayed in Canaan his family would probably have become absorbed in the Canaanite culture and would never have become a nation. The similarity between Canaanite culture and Jacob's family made this a distinct possibility. But there was no possibility of this in Egypt because the Egyptians themselves loathed shepherds (Gen. 46:34).

We need only to turn to the first chapter of Exodus to see how completely God fulfilled this promise. There we encounter these words: 'But the children of Israel were fruitful and increased abundantly, multiplied and grew exceedingly mighty; and the land was filled with them' (Exod. 1:7).

So God had it all worked out in advance. Joseph was sold into slavery in Egypt so that God could in due time raise him up as ruler in that land and he, Joseph, could then bring all his people there. God is sovereign. His will is never thwarted or circumvented. What appears to be a defeat for him is but one more step in his relentless march to victory.

God's presence

Secondly, the Lord promised to be present with Jacob in Egypt. He said to Jacob, 'I will go down with you to Egypt...' (v. 4).

Matthew Henry writes: 'Those that go whither God sends them shall certainly have God with them, and that is enough to secure them wherever they are and to silence their fears; we may safely venture even into Egypt if God go down with us.'[1]

George Lawson adds: 'The chief pleasure of Jacob in the land of Canaan was, that God was with him in all his sojournings... But the presence of God was not confined to the land of promise ... God promised to be with him in the way in which he was now going, and in the country to which he was going. No enemies would be able to destroy him; no accident to deprive him of the possession of his soul; no death to terrify him, if God was with him. We may walk, not only with safety, but with joy, through the valley of the shadow of death if God be with us. Though our heart and our flesh fail us, God will be the strength of our hearts and our portion for ever. How blessed was Jacob, having such a promise as this to sweeten all his trials! But have not all Christians the same promise to cheer their spirits under every trial?'[2]

Removal from Egypt

Thirdly, the Lord promised to bring Jacob out of Egypt (v. 4). This promise included both an individual and national aspect. The individual aspect was fulfilled when Jacob's sons brought his body back to the land of Canaan for burial (Gen. 50:12-13). The national aspect was fulfilled when his descendants came out of Egypt under the leadership of Moses.

Unbroken fellowship

Finally, the Lord promised that Jacob would never again be deprived of Joseph (v. 4). Jacob had been without Joseph for many years. How often his heart ached during those years! But he would never know that ache again. Joseph would be with him all the remaining years of his life and would be there with him when he died. We may wonder why God would promise this to Jacob after depriving him of Joseph's presence for more than twenty years. George Lawson says, 'We must not pretend to penetrate the depth of Divine counsels. God withholds at one time that consolation from His people of which they stood in great need, and at other times gives them an extraordinary measure of consolation. But it would be a great error to suppose that the ways of God are unequal. He has always good reasons for what He does, although He is never bound to tell us what they are, and does not always, in this world, think fit to inform us.'[3]

Bible students have long viewed Joseph as one of the most striking of all the types of Christ. We do well to regard him as such at this particular point. Each believer may rest assured that the Lord Jesus Christ will 'put his hand' on his eyes. And when the believer opens his eyes on the other side of death, it will be to see his Christ in all his glory.

Life sometimes presents God's people with daunting challenges as it did Jacob. But we can face them all with peace if we remember God's tender concern for his people, his faithfulness to them and his sweet promises.

15.
Reunion day

Genesis 46:28-30

These verses present us with one of the most tender and moving scenes in all the Bible. Here Jacob and Joseph meet after more than twenty years of being separated. Who can comprehend the joy they felt on this occasion?

Jacob's heart most certainly ached with a deep void during those years of separation, years he spent thinking his son was dead. Joseph's heart most certainly felt the pain as well. But the anguish of those long years of separation evaporated as they embraced. By the way, every single child of God can say the same of his believing loved ones as Jacob said about Joseph, namely, he is 'still alive' (45:28). George Lawson writes: 'Our friends who have died in the Lord are yet alive. They live with God in heaven. We cannot go and see them before we die. But as soon as we die, we shall go and see them, and to see Christ, which is far better, and to dwell with them and with Him for ever and ever.'[1]

There are several moving reunions in the Bible. Jacob himself had two memorable ones before being reunited with Joseph. The first was with his brother Esau (Gen. 33:4), the second was with his father Isaac (35:27). We also cannot help but think of David's reunion with Jonathan (1 Sam. 23:16-18) and the prodigal son's with his father (Luke 15:11-24).

There have been countless heart-warming reunions between family members and friends down through the centuries. But the best of all reunions lies ahead. That is when believers in Jesus Christ will be reunited with their believing loved ones. The apostle Paul gives us insight into this reunion in his letter to the Thessalonians (1 Thess. 4:13-18).

Some of the features of Jacob's reunion with Joseph will no doubt be present in that glorious reunion. From the time he learned that Joseph was alive, Jacob undoubtedly experienced something of these features. But they hit him with full force when he and Joseph met.

Understanding

At that indescribable moment, we may assume that understanding flooded over Jacob. What had seemed so mysterious and inexplicable to him had all become perfectly clear.

Years before, when he saw Joseph's bloody garment, Jacob assumed his beloved son had been devoured by beasts (37:31-35). Imagine the thoughts that went racing through his head at that time. Why would God let such a thing happen?

We know some things that Jacob did not know at that time, namely, that Joseph was still alive and that Jacob's other sons were responsible for his disappearance. But we also know that God could have prevented the evil plot of Joseph's brothers. God was not sitting by helplessly when Joseph was sold into slavery. While he, God, was not responsible for the evil of Joseph's brothers, he permitted them to carry it out.

Why? Because he had a plan. As Jacob stood there staring at the bloody garment handed to him, he could only see his own tiny slice of reality. He had no way of knowing about God's larger plan, a plan by which he would put Joseph in a position of authority in Egypt so that he, Joseph, could settle all his family members in a place where they could grow into a nation.

As Jacob embraced his son, he had some insight into this plan, and he must have stood in awe of it. Had we been there to ask his assessment of the way God had dealt with him, he might very well have said, 'God has done all things well.'

God's people often find themselves facing difficult and mysterious circumstances. We easily identify with the words:

> Trials dark on every hand
> And we cannot understand,
> All the ways that God would lead us
> To that blessed promised land.[2]

On that reunion day our bewilderment will vanish. On that day when our Lord Jesus comes to gather us to himself and to rejoin us to our believing loved ones, all the mists of life will clear and we will be lost in 'wonder, love and praise'. It will be our united testimony on that day that God made no mistakes in his dealings with us, that he had a kind and benevolent purpose even in those circumstances that seared us with pain. We see now through a glass darkly, but then face to face (1 Cor. 13:12). And when we finally see clearly, we will also say, 'God has done all things well.'

A twinge of regret

I cannot help but think that Jacob had to feel more than a twinge of regret when he and Joseph met. He may very well have found his thoughts gravitating to that time, years before, when Joseph shared a dream with him that he, Jacob, would bow before Joseph (Gen. 37:9-11).

Jacob 'kept the matter in mind' (Gen. 37:11), but he failed to hear in that dream the Word of God. He should have heard it because he himself had received that Word through dreams; but he did not. If Jacob had detected the Word of God in Joseph's dreams, he would not have abandoned all hope that his son was still alive. He would have said something like this to himself: 'I do not know how, but my son has to be alive in order for the Word of God to be fulfilled.'

When the people of God finally enter into heavenly glory, there will be a moment when God will wipe every tear from their eyes. But before that moment, it may very well be that each one will feel keen regret that throughout life he did not trust the Word of God more fully. When we see the glory of our Lord, we might say to ourselves: 'O ... slow of heart to believe...' (Luke 24:25).

If we want to feel no regret on that day, we must trust and obey the Word of God on this and every day.

A new life in a new place

There was yet another dimension to Jacob's reunion with Joseph. It meant for Jacob a new life in a new place. Old things had passed away for him. All things were now new. He would never live in Canaan again.

We have no difficulty at all in applying Jacob's experience of newness in Egypt to what lies ahead of believers in Jesus Christ. Oh, what newness awaits them on their glad reunion day! On that day the Lord Jesus Christ will return from heaven's glory. Dead believers will be raised to meet him in the air. Living believers will be changed instantaneously and caught up to meet them in the air. And all this will culminate in those believers entering into eternal glory in heaven. They will not be raised and reunited so that they can resume life in this world. Who would want that? Who would want to come back to this world with its trials and sufferings? The poor reincarnationist thinks he will have come back to this vale of tears again and again. We can be thankful that this is not the case! The people of God are not raised to oldness but to new-ness. They will have new lives in a new place.

Those new lives will be lived in new bodies. The aches and pains of these bodies will be banished for ever. Sickness will be no more. Death itself will have died. There will be no sad funeral processions in heaven; no obituary columns; no cemeteries.

On that day every saint will have a body that is fashioned after the body the Lord Jesus Christ now has. The apostle Paul puts it like this: 'For our citizenship is in heaven, from which we also eagerly wait for the Saviour, the Lord Jesus Christ, who will transform our lowly body that it may be con-formed to his glorious body, according to the working by which he is able even to subdue all things to himself' (Phil. 3:20-21).

And what about this new place? What will it be like? The apostle John was given a breathtaking preview of it by the Lord Jesus himself. John says, 'Now I saw a new heaven and a new earth, for the first heaven and the first earth had passed away. Also there was no more sea. Then I, John, saw the holy city, New Jerusalem, coming down out of heaven from God, prepared as a bride adorned for her husband' (Rev. 21:1-2).

The final state for the believer will not be floating around on a cloud up there somewhere. No, it will be on this earth, which will then be restored to the beauty and glory it had before sin entered. If we can find much to like in this world now, with all the havoc created by sin, we will be thrilled beyond belief by the new earth, which will be free from sin.

The new earth will have only one city, the heavenly city. It will be beautiful beyond compare. The apostle John writes:

'Then one of the seven angels ... carried me away in the Spirit to a great and high mountain, and showed me the great city, the holy Jerusalem, descending out of heaven from God, having the glory of God. Her light was like a most precious stone, like a jasper stone, clear as crystal' (Rev. 21:9-11).

From that point the Apostle proceeds to describe the gates, the wall and the foundation of the city. What a place it will be! And there the saints will spend eternity. But the marvellous thing about eternity in heaven is that it cannot be spent. When we have been there ten thousand years, we will have no less days to sing God's praise than when we first began.

The most important and urgent business in all of life is to make sure we do not miss the reunion day of the saints and the glories that will follow. But, tragedy of tragedies, many will miss it. They will miss the glories of heaven and will face an eternity of misery and woe.

The good news of the Bible is that those who want to share in the delights of eternal glory can do so. There is a way to heaven. It is through the redeeming work of God's Son. The call goes out from the pages of Scripture for each of us to repent of our sins and to trust completely in Christ. My plea to each one who has not heeded this call is very simple — heed it today.

16.
Thinking about home

Genesis 47:7-10, 27-31; 48:15-16, 21-22

Jacob spent the last seventeen years of his life in Egypt. As we read the account of those years, we cannot help but get the impression that he spent a large proportion of his time thinking about his home.

We are only partly right if we take that to mean that Jacob thought a lot about the land of Canaan. We may be sure that he did. But we know that the patriarchs looked beyond the land of Canaan to a better land, the land of heaven. The author of Hebrews says of Abraham: 'By faith he dwelt in the land of promise as in a foreign country, dwelling in tents with Isaac and Jacob, the heirs with him of the same promise; for he waited for the city which has foundations, whose builder and maker is God' (Heb. 11:9-10, see also Heb. 11:13-16). When I say Jacob spent his last years thinking about home, I am referring primarily to his heavenly home.

The Bible calls us to be heavenly-minded, but few of us seem to be excelling in this area. We are concerned that we are not thought to be so heavenly-minded that we are of no earthly good. We have forgotten that the Bible teaches just the opposite. The most heavenly-minded do the most good on this earth.

We need to examine the account of Jacob's last years and learn from him to think often about our heavenly home. As we study this account, we find four truths emerging.

Convinced of God's faithfulness

First, we cannot think about home unless we are convinced of God's faithfulness. We have only one warrant for thinking about our heavenly home. God has promised that there is such a place! If God is not trustworthy and reliable, we cannot be sure that heaven awaits us. But if God is faithful, we may eagerly look forward to heaven.

How can we be assured that God is faithful? The answer is that God has given us many evidences of his faithfulness. He has demonstrated it again and again. If we want to see the faithfulness of God, we only have to look back.

Jacob knew about God's faithfulness. There were too many evidences for him to think otherwise. He received one such evidence when his son Joseph introduced him to Pharaoh. What a riveting and surprising scene! Here is Jacob, an ordinary shepherd, standing before Pharaoh, king of Egypt. The chasm between shepherd and king was enormous. It was especially so in this case because Egyptians loathed shepherds (46:34).

Even more surprising is the nature of the meeting between Jacob and Pharaoh. If we did not have this account of the meeting and had only tried to picture it in our minds, we probably would have seen Jacob occupying the inferior position. We would have seen Pharaoh as dominant and Jacob coming before him in something of a cringing, fawning manner.

But Jacob is dominant in this passage. Pharaoh does not bless Jacob; Jacob blesses Pharaoh. In fact he blesses him when he enters (v. 7) and when he departs (v. 10). The blesser is obviously superior to the one blessed!

How did Jacob come to occupy this superior position? Pharaoh was obviously impressed with his age. He had probably never before seen anyone so old, and he could not wait to ask Jacob's age. But the ultimate explanation is that God was at work in this situation. While Jacob's age caused Pharaoh to be deferential towards him, it was merely an instrument in God's hand.

And what was the Lord doing through Jacob's interview with Pharaoh? Jacob himself may not have realized it at the time, but his meeting with Pharaoh served as one tiny fulfilment of the promise that God had made to Abraham. When the Lord called Abraham into a special covenant relationship with himself, he said,

'And in you all the families
of the earth shall be blessed'

(Gen. 12:3).

Here now is Abraham's grandson pronouncing a blessing on Pharaoh. The head of the covenant nation pronounces a blessing on the head of another nation, and God's promise is partially fulfilled. That partial fulfilment served as a guarantee of the ultimate fulfilment which is, of course, in the Lord Jesus Christ who came from Abraham's family. Through Christ 'all the families of the earth' have been blessed either with the saving knowledge of Christ or with the benefits produced by that knowledge.

On the basis of what he had seen of the faithfulness of God in his life, Jacob could assure Joseph that the Lord could be trusted to do what he had promised (48:21). God's people can think about their heavenly home because God has promised it to them and he never breaks a promise.

Thinking differently about life in this world

Secondly, we cannot think about home without it having a transforming effect on how we view this life. We can put it like this — thinking about our heavenly home helps us see through this life.

His response to Pharaoh indicates that he, Jacob, had thought enough about his heavenly home to see that this life is but a brief pilgrimage. When Pharaoh asked his age, Jacob said, '...few and evil have been the days of the years of my life, and they have not attained to the days of the years of the life of my fathers in the days of their pilgrimage' (47:9). In other words, Jacob did not view this world as an end in and of itself. He saw it as a travelling-place, not a stopping-place; as a highway to a destination, not the destination itself.

Countless multitudes fail to see what Jacob did. As far as they are concerned, this world is all there is, and they have to wring out of it every bit of enjoyment they possibly can. Death is the ultimate tragedy for these people because it is the end of the only life there is. How much happier are those who share Jacob's view! This life is very important, but it is only a prelude to the far better life awaiting those who know God through the saving work of his Son, Jesus Christ.

Praising God as our shepherd

Jacob's thinking about home teaches us a third truth, that is, we cannot think about home without praising God as our shepherd (48:15-16).

We 'fast forward' now to the very end of Jacob's life. On hearing that his father was very ill, Joseph took his two sons, Ephraim and Manasseh, to visit him. In the process of

pronouncing blessings on Joseph's sons, Jacob spoke these
words:

'The God who has fed me
   all my life long to this day,
The Angel who has redeemed
   me from all evil,
Bless the lads...'

(48:15-16).

As we have noted, Jacob regarded this life as a journey. That
journey was now almost over, and he would soon be entering
the presence of the Lord. Realizing this, Jacob pauses to look
back over the path he had trodden. What twists and turns he
had seen! There were many times when his circumstances
made no sense at all to him and he undoubtedly thought that
God had forgotten him. But as Jacob looked back, he realized that the Lord had been there all along, not as a mere
passive observer but as an active shepherd (the word 'fed'
should be translated 'shepherd'). The Lord had been to Jacob
everything a shepherd is to his sheep. He had provided and
guided, protected and sustained.

Each child of God must surely come to the end of life with
the keen awareness that he has had a shepherd. That shepherd, the Lord Jesus Christ (John 10:11-30), made him part
of his flock and has provided, guided, protected and sustained
him all through life. Even in those moments of dark despair,
when the child of God thought he was utterly alone, the Lord
was there shepherding him.

Here is how good the good shepherd is — he will finally
shepherd all his sheep home to glory, and when they arrive,
there will be no doubt in their minds that he led them all the
way.

Leaving a spiritual legacy

That brings us to a final point. We cannot think about home without desiring to leave a spiritual legacy.

Jacob did not come to the end of his journey as a mere victim of circumstances. He used the last precious hours of his life to bless the sons of Joseph (47:15-20) and to offer prophecies regarding his own sons (49:1-27).

Those who know the truth about heaven will never be content to go there without taking others along with them. They will be particularly concerned about leaving a spiritual legacy with their own children. If at all possible, they will use the last hours of life to talk to their children about:

- their faith and why they hold it
- their life and how they made it
- their hope and how they prize it

May God help those of us who know him to think much about heaven these days, reminding ourselves that this life is only a journey to a far better place. Let us praise him as we journey and seek to urge others to journey with us.

17.
Dying faith

Genesis 49:8-12

Knowing it was time for him to die, Jacob gathered his sons together for the purpose of giving them insight into the future. While each of these prophecies contains much of interest, it is immediately obvious that the one pertaining to Judah is quite different. It stands head and shoulders above the rest. Jacob himself signalled the special nature of his prophecy regarding Judah:

> 'Judah, you are he whom
> your brothers shall praise...'
>
> (v. 8).

The reason for this became clear as Jacob continued. Judah would be the tribe from which the Messiah would come.

Jacob most certainly felt exhilarated that he was able to speak these words! His faith was in that coming Messiah, and the fact that he, Jacob, spoke as he did means that God had given him additional information about the Messiah. We cannot say it too often. The people of the Old Testament were all saved in exactly the same way as we are, that is, through the redeeming work of the Lord Jesus Christ (John 8:56; Acts 10:43; 1 Peter 1:10-12). They looked forward in faith to Christ, while we look backward. But there is salvation only in Christ. No one will be in heaven except through him.

We look at Jacob's prophecy regarding Judah, then, because we share the faith of Jacob, faith in the Messiah of God. And we look at it because the salvation provided by Christ is so very important and crucial that it is impossible for us to give too much attention to it. Jacob's prophecy may very well give us additional insight into the mission of Christ. It presents three aspects of his saving work.

The lion and his prey (vv. 8-9).

When a lion takes his prey, nothing disturbs or distracts him. The lion does not have to worry about some other animal coming along and taking the prey from him. He eats his fill and might even pause in his feeding to take a nap. Who is going to take prey from a lion?

What a precious truth there is here! We can say legitimately that the Lord Jesus Christ came to this earth to claim his prey. Just as the lion has his prey as the primary focus and object of his life, so Christ came to this earth with a very definite object and purpose in mind, namely, to go to the cross of Calvary and there purchase salvation for all who believe. Oh, how the devil tried to deter Christ from pursuing that object! Three times he tempted him in the wilderness, but Jesus stood firm (Matt. 4:1-11).

There was that occasion when the Lord Jesus fed 5000 in the wilderness, and the people wanted to make him their king (John 6:14-15). That might sound innocent enough, but it constituted nothing less than an attempt of the devil to persuade Jesus to set up his kingdom without dying on the cross.

On the night before our Lord was crucified, he spoke these words to his disciples: '...the ruler of this world is coming, and he has nothing in me' (John 14:30). Jesus knew that Satan would be, as it were, on the prowl that very evening, making a desperate attempt to deter him from going to the cross. But the victory was secure. There was nothing in Jesus for Satan to work with. There was nothing there except complete fidelity and devotion to the Father who had set the cross before him.

Satan did not stop even when Jesus was on the cross. He prompted the religious leaders to say, 'He saved others; let him save himself if he is the Christ, the chosen of God' (Luke 23:35). One of the two thieves with whom he was crucified said, 'If you are the Christ, save yourself and us' (Luke 23:39).

Even the cup offered to Jesus while he was on the cross was a further temptation. That cup, consisting of 'sour wine mingled with gall' (Matt. 27:34), was intended to deaden the pain. Jesus refused it. He had to experience fully the sufferings of Calvary.

Why was it so very important for Jesus to go to that cross, and, once there, to stay until he died? Would it have been so terrible if he had bypassed the cross? Yes, it would have been absolutely catastrophic for us, because Jesus' death on that cross was the way God had selected to provide salvation for sinners.

You see, his death there was not just another man dying another death. It was a special death, a death in which Jesus actually received the wrath of God against believing sinners. Because he took that wrath in their stead, there is no wrath left for them. How we should praise God that Jesus, like the lion, was not deterred from his prey! Nothing drove him away. He stayed with it until his task was completed, and when that time came he cried out in victory: 'It is finished!' (John 19:30).

The Lord Jesus is now seated at the right hand of God. He is there as a conqueror. No one can unseat or defeat him.

The rightful ruler (v. 10).

The word 'Shiloh' has sparked considerable debate. Some suggest it means 'son'. Others say the meaning is 'sent'. Some believe that it means 'peace'. Still others say it means 'the one to whom it belongs'.

We are in a very happy position because we have no trouble at all seeing Christ in each one of these suggestions. He is the Son of God and the Son of Man. He was sent by the Father to perform the work of redemption. By performing that work, he produces peace between God and sinners.

It appears, however, that the context favours the last suggestion, that is, 'the one to whom it belongs'. Jacob was prophesying that the tribe of Judah would be the one from which the nation's rulers would come. Beginning with David, the tribe of Judah would provide rulers for the nation until the Lord Jesus came. Even when the Jews were under the control of other nations, they had some sort of governor.

While rule would characterize the tribe of Judah it would not reach its fullest extent or degree until Shiloh. Walter Kaiser says, '...the idea is that the sovereignty of Judah is brought to its highest point under the arrival and rule of Shiloh'.[1]

Christ is the pre-eminent ruler. He is the one to whom all the rulers of Israel were intended to point. Her best-known rulers, David and Solomon, were only very faint representations of the power and glory of the Lord Jesus.

Jacob's prophecy also includes these words: 'And to him shall be the obedience of the people' (v. 10). Christ came to this earth for the express purpose of delivering his people from their sins and to secure their obedience to himself. Those who do not render obedience to Christ only give evidence that they do not really know him. No Christian obeys perfectly, but every Christian sincerely acknowledges Christ as his rightful ruler, agrees that his laws are just and right, desires to obey those laws, and mourns when he fails in obedience.

Because Christ is now enthroned in heaven above and reigning in the hearts of his people, it is not easy to detect his rule. But this phase of his kingship will soon give way to a reign that will be evident to, and acknowledged by, all. What a day that will be!

The beautiful one who produces bounty for his people (vv. 11-12).

These verses have proved difficult to interpret. Jacob speaks of the Messiah binding his donkey to the vine, washing his garments in wine, having eyes that are darker than wine, and teeth whiter than milk.

These four phrases fall naturally into two parts. The first two phrases make the same point about the Messiah. The next two make a further point about him. The first two phrases depict the fruitfulness of the land during the time of the Messiah.

- 'binding his donkey to the vine'. Gerhard Charles Aalders applies it to the Messiah in this way: 'The figure used here seems to indicate that in His day grapevines ... would be so abundant that they could be used for other purposes. Even the choicest vines could be used for hitching posts. Thus, the figure denoted a time of exceptional fruitfulness.'[2]

- 'washing his garments in wine'. This is yet another expression of abundance. Wine would be so plentiful that one could wash his garments in it. Aalders exclaims: 'What a graphic picture of abundance and even excess!'[3]

We should not be surprised that the land of Judah would abound in fruitfulness in the time of Jesus. It would only be proper for the natural realm to welcome its Creator by yielding an abundance. And the fruitfulness of the natural order served as a fitting emblem for the spiritual fruitfulness Jesus provided through his work of redemption (John 10:10; Eph. 1:3-14).

The next two phrases point to the beauty of the Messiah. Dark eyes and white teeth were highly valued as marks of beauty. The Messiah would prove to be beautiful to his people because of the salvation he would provide.

Jacob's prophecy concerning Judah tells us that the old patriarch went to his grave thinking about the coming Christ. He pinned all his hopes on Christ as the mighty lion, the rightful ruler and the one devoted to his people. There is no better way to die than this.

Notes

Introduction
1. Quoted by John MacArthur, *In the Footsteps of Faith*, Crossway Books, p.7.
2. As above.

Chapter 2: The 'Esau flaw'
1. This chapter has been published under the title 'Esau: a warning against living for the present' in my book *How to live in a dangerous world*, Evangelical Press, pp.23-8.
2. Quoted by Warren W. Wiersbe, *Treasury of the World's Great Sermons*, Kregel Publications, p.40.

Chapter 3: Inadequate responses to the Word of God
1. S. G. DeGraaf, *Promise and Deliverance*, Paideia Press, vol. i, p.174.
2. As above, p.187.

Chapter 4: Jacob's dream at Bethel
1. Cited by Don Fortner in a sermon entitled 'Jacob's Ladder', 30. 11. 99.
2. Robert A. Laidlaw, *The Reason Why*, World Bible Publishers, pp.11-2.
3. Matthew Henry, *Matthew Henry's Commentary*, Fleming H. Revell Publishing Company, vol. 1, p.172.

Chapter 5: Jacob in God's school
1. J. I. Packer, *Knowing God*, InterVarsity Press, p.84.
2. As above.

Chapter 6: Glimpses of grace
1. From the hymn 'All the way my Saviour leads me'.

Chapter 7: When Esau comes
1. A. W. Pink, *Gleanings in Genesis*, Moody Press, p.284.
2. As above, p.285.

Chapter 8: Jacob and the heavenly wrestler
1. Packer, *Knowing God*, p.85.

Chapter 9: Important truths
1. James Montgomery Boice, *Genesis*, Baker Book House, vol. ii, p.824.
2. Pink, *Gleanings*, p.298.
3. Boice, *Genesis*, vol. ii, p.824.
4. From the hymn 'Grace, 'tis a charming sound', *A Selection of Hymns for Public Worship* by William Gadsby, The Gospel Standard Societies, 1991.

Chapter 10: An ugly and sordid episode
1. Quoted by Boice, *Genesis*, vol. ii, p.829.

Chapter 14: Sweet consolations for the challenges of life
1. Henry, *Commentary*, vol. i, p.248.
2. George Lawson, *The Life of Joseph*, The Banner of Truth, p.313.
3. As above, p.316.

Chapter 15: Reunion day
1. Lawson, *Joseph*, p.303.
2. From the hymn 'When the morning comes', by Charles A. Tindley.

Chapter 17: Dying faith
1. Walter C. Kaiser Jr, Peter H. Davids, F. F. Bruce, Manfred T. Brauch, *Hard Sayings of the Bible*, InterVarsity Press, p.134.
2. Gerhard Charles Aalders, *Bible Student Commentary: Genesis*, vol. i, p.280.
3. As above.

Other books from the author:

Faithful under fire

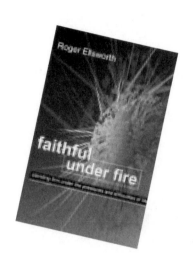

The life of Joseph is a compelling source of encouragement for Christians who find themselves confronted with the pressures of daily living. Joseph's message to them is clear: look to God's promises and draw strength from them. God can, through these promises, enable us to endure the arrows of affliction that fly our way and even to respond with the arrows of kindness, patience and faith.

But Joseph not only demonstrated what it means to live in dependence on God's Word, he also clearly foreshadowed the life and work of the Lord Jesus Christ in a way that provides further confirmation of the utter reliability of God's Word and his promises.

In his suffering and eventual exaltation to a position where he was able to 'save many people alive', Joseph points us to the Saviour who willingly endured a far greater humiliation in order to save his people.

Faithful under fire, Roger Ellsworth, ISBN 0 85234 351 5, 128 pages, published by Evangelical Press.

The Guide — the Bible book by book

The Bible book by book is the first in a new series of publications called The Guide. This book provides a complete overview of the Bible, divided into fifty-two chapters, which is ideal for use as a resource for a group Bible study or on an individual basis. It covers every book of the Bible, giving both its historical and spiritual significance, and shows how each individual book fits into God's perfect plan for his people throughout history.

The aim of The Guide series is to communicate the Christian faith in a straightforward and readable way, and to that end each chapter is relatively short and concise, but also contains questions for further study. An innovative feature of the series is that it is linked to its own web site, which can be found at www.evangelicalpress.org, where further questions may be posted, to be answered by a team of experienced dedicated men.

The Bible book by book, Roger Ellsworth, ISBN 0852344864, 432 pages, published by Evangelical Press.

How to live in a dangerous world

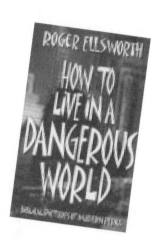

Our televisions and newspapers bombard us with dangers threatening our economy, our environment, our educational system and more, but the greatest dangers we face are spiritual ones.

The dangers which worry us the most are often able to damage us only here and now, but mistaken beliefs can lead to eternal ruin.

Roger Ellsworth identifies many of the major beliefs and values of our day, finds Bible characters who shared the same perspectives and discovers where those beliefs and values led them. The author wants to know what we may learn from those who have gone before us and how we may avoid falling into the same pitfalls as they did. The result is a fresh understanding of the grace of God which enabled others to overcome the very real dangers they faced and which is still more than sufficient for every one of us living in our dangerous world.

How to live in a dangerous world, ISBN 0 85234 416 3, 256 pages, published by Evangelical Press.

From the Welwyn Commentary series
published by Evangelical Press

Apostasy, destruction and hope
2 Kings simply explained
ISBN 0 85234 510 0
272 pages

From glory to ruin

Study of 1 Kings
ISBN 0 85234 451 1
256 pages

*Strengthening
Christ's church*
The message of 1 Corinthians
ISBN 0 85234 333 7
272 pages

A wide range of excellent books on spiritual subjects is available from Evangelical Press. Please write to us for your free catalogue or contact us by e-mail.

Evangelical Press
Faverdale North Industrial Estate, Darlington, DL3 0PH, England

Evangelical Press USA
P. O. Box 84, Auburn, MA 01501, USA

e-mail: sales@evangelicalpress.org

web: www.evangelicalpress.org